DROP
EFFECT

DROP EFFECT

Drop Effect is the book that creates a new dimension in perceiving the ways of predicting and managing the changes.

MILAN DIMITRIJEVIC

Library of Congress Control Number:		2011913145
ISBN:	Hardcover	978-1-4653-0296-0
	Softcover	978-1-4653-0295-3
	Ebook	978-1-4653-0297-7

This book was printed in the United States of America.

To order additional copies of this book, contact:
Xlibris Corporation
0-800-644-6988
www.xlibrispublishing.co.uk
Orders@xlibrispublishing.co.uk
302504

Table of Contents

DEDICATION

Behind each ordinary man, there is an extraordinary story.
Each extraordinary story is followed by ordinary mistakes.
That is life.

Drop effect is my life story, story of an ordinary man. It's intended to everyone, it's written for a better tomorrow, for the wellbeing of all of us.

PROLOGUE

Dear readers, I would like to thank you for sparing some time to read my thoughts. *Drop Effect* is written in simple language, and I hope, it is easy to read. This book is created for everyone, but especially for business people, like owners of companies, employees in companies, entrepreneurs, managers, innovators, leaders and all those who think that there's no one smarter than them. It is incredible how much ignorance can heart and cost, but we rarely admit that we are wrong or that we are making a mistake.

The book contents are the experiences of everyday situations, as well as my opinions on different experiences from the world corporations and leaders to the everyday people's experiences. The purpose of this book is to show you the potential mistakes in business and life, which you could have made, but luckily for you, you found the book on time. I had a lot of trouble cooling down my rebellious nature (some say I'm still fighting, which is true), that resulted with never ending mistakes, which cost one twenty-eight year old, millions of dollars, and probably years and years of life.

I know, I know, you probably think, here is another bighead who things he's a guru in consulting, he had earned a couple of bucks, and now he things he has learned all the life lessons. Unfortunately, I must disappoint you, but it is not like that. Indeed, I use to consider myself this way, until I hit the bottom, and that, in every meaning of the word; it had made me realize that sometimes I have to stop and listen to wise people's advices.

Probably you won't find all the life and business lessons in this book, but you will find some useful advices that will help you not to make the same mistakes that I did, which is much better, since this book costs at least ten thousand or million times less than the unexpected expenses would cost you if you made my mistakes.

Ok, the first part of the introduction is mainly clear, but many people were asking, even during the creation of the book, why is it entitled *Drop Effect*, what is hiding behind that title? Actually, behind the title, there are stories and advices that can be helpful in many ways, especially in predicting and managing the changes. It's very simple; please just concentrate.

Imagine turning on the tap to fill the glass with water. In the most cases, the glass will fill up with water and some drops will fall outside of it, perhaps because of the stronger stream, or your negligence, but it happens almost every single time, no matter how careful you are. Those situations, you'd agree, almost don't have any further consequences that would demand spending great time on cleaning and swabbing the water, since those small accidental drops are so imperceptible and negligible. You can compare this situation with companies, leaders, individuals who have organized their life in such a manner that they can have only problems in the size of that drop.

On the other hand, imagine turning on the tap to fill up the glass with water, only this time, let us assume your hand gets on the top of the glass and prevents the water from filling the glass. Naturally, the damage is much bigger than in the first case, the drops are everywhere around us, and in the blink of an eye a set of new problems is emerging. You can compare these situations with companies, leaders, individuals who have organized their life in such a manner that with inattention, ignorance and lack of concentration, they can create the flood of drops (a crisis situation) just from the small drops (negligible, everyday problems).

The drops represent the expected and even more the unexpected problems, and their quantity best presents your level of organization and concentration. If you don't have too many drops, then you are very well organized, while if you have a flood of drops, then you are facing big problems. Yes, Gentlemen, it is like that, but don't waste your time looking for the perpetrator, just look in the mirror and you'll have the solution: you are the perpetrator, because you left your rebellious nature and your bad organization make the flood of drops, and the flood damages are always huge.

Let me get to the point. Companies and individuals not having many drops are rare. The drops are present everywhere, which is why it is crucial to invest all your energy to predict and prevent the creation of the flood and the general chaos. It is incredible how the drops can direct our life. It took me much time to realize it, but the time has come to join our forces, and stop the drops from having control of us, instead we must take control over them, and organize our lives so that every drop travels in the direction that we determinate.

I hope you take good advantage of my experiences and advices. Enjoy.

Milan Dimitrijevic

1

DOES FAMILY COME FIRST?

Does your family come first? You probably find this question strange, and deep inside, I know that you think the same way as I do: "Yes, my family comes first, and now what?" How good are you in that, do you commit enough time to your family, do you spend playing with your children at least the half of the energy that you spend at work? I know, the most of you avoid this topic or think that they're the perfect parents, but for a moment—let's get back to reality.

For example, me, I am far from being a perfect parent. As I already mentioned before, I have a rebellious nature and I never liked listening to others, things that specially affected my family. Believe it or not, I am 28 years old (as I write this book); I have three marriages behind me and two children with different wives. My older daughter was born in my second marriage, and the younger one in the third. Now, you probably think, how did he have the time for three marriages, he probably never worked, he was only changing wives and making children. I know how all this may sound to you, but lets get to the point.

Can you imagine how people look at me and what they think about me when they hear all this? Does this person do anything else in life except getting married and making children?

Yes, this person does many things, but also makes children and gets married. A good divorce is a much better solution than a bad marriage. The first divorce went well, the second one was horrible, and I still didn't get divorced from my third wife. I have two wonderful daughters that I love very much, and I daily tell it to them. Of course, they are still very young to understand the whole situation and the kind of father they have. Ok, I think we explained pretty well this, not so bright side of my *Drop Effect* part of life, now is the time for the consequences of my failed marriages, or for the drops, whatever you prefer.

My dear Friends, actually, not everything is as dark as it seems. Many would, in my place, finish up in those institutions where hands don't have that much of a liberty (because of the tight shirt, of course), but the good thing is that I realized very early where I'd made a mistake. The family represents the foundation of your future successes therefore, it is necessary to be built solid. Making a family is a serious thing, very quickly, your children will become your copies, and then it would be too late to ask yourself if you made a mistake and where did you make one. I did many things without taking time to think, blame it on my young age, on my ignorance, on my rebellious nature, etc.

Either way, I have no excuses for my behavior towards my family. Creating a family could never be compared to building a company. Why did I say that? In business, you will make yourself another chance, but in the family life—one false movement can have enormous consequences.

In my case, the consequences were big; I lost a lot of time on the wrong things. In the meanwhile the one who suffered the most was my older daughter, she was not seeing me on regularly bases, I postponed almost all my work obligations, and I didn't care even if everything was about to be lost. All I felt was anger, anxiety, apathy and constantly—the lack of air. Do you know why lack of air? Because I was surrounded by a flood of drops, a flood of bad decisions, which resulted with even worse decisions, and worse and worse . . . Of course all this is over, now I like to say, "All this is going to be a yesterday, everything passes". The consequences were too big and there was almost no way out.

I also had my parents' example, they are married for more than thirty years, but you usually don't see what is in front of your nose. My father's wisdom and stability were results of his good marriage, not of good business. Once he told me, women are the reason for the biggest wars in history; the woman needs to be conquered, you must fight for her, you need to do everything to make the woman that you love be yours, and then, when you

conquer her, be a fool (he refers to my rebellious nature), and make her go away. He spoke wisely, so much trouble to win someone and then to let her go. That's a big mistake.

These days, the biggest problem of the contemporary way of doing business is harmonizing the family and the business obligations. Maybe some will not agree with me, but try to think how many times did it happen that you stayed longer at work, how many times didn't you take your child from the school, etc, and you'll see that I'm right.

Dear Gentlemen, being a good father, mother, husband, or wife is the most difficult job of your life. The life lessons regarding this subject can't be learned in the famous business school, you must cope with them alone, learning from your own mistakes.

You have to devote more time to your family. I know that you would like to be big, rich, powerful, successful and blah, blah, blah . . . My dear Friends, being big is a complex concept, and we'll all agree that for achieving big goals, big sacrifices are needed. During your efforts and pursuits of the big accomplishments, somewhere between the lines in your life, there's someone for whom you are always the best and the biggest, and those are you children, your family.

Children smile, the naïve look in their eyes, as well as their joy when they see you, is most sincere thing that you have in your life. You need to be careful how you spend your time, because the smiles can turn into the tears, and you'll get all kind of looks except the naïve ones.

So, what do you think, did I make enough mistakes to learn how should I treat the family and its values?

My house and family represent the foundation of everything I have and represent. Depending on my decisions, the future will show if the foundation will support the future upgrade of personal success and failures. I've admitted it, I am not perfect when it comes to committing time to my children, but I do try very hard for them not to feel my absence.

Can you take some good advices from this story?

I'll try to help you. Here are some advices:

THE FAMILY MUST COME FIRST, NO COMPROMISES ACCEPTED.

(The image of stable, family man will never be questioned, in many cases this could be the key characteristic in your business. First, it is important

that you don't lie to yourself by constantly saying that family comes first, instead make it happen, without any compromises or delay, the resultants will be magnificent.)

DON'T BRAG ABOUT BEING A GOOD PARENT, YOUR CHILDREN'S RESULTS WILL BEST PROVE IT.

(Only time will tell, through your children's results, if you're a good parent. Of course, also the environment has a very big influence on our children, but that influence is something that comes from the outside of your home, and it comes as an actual upgrade to the behavioral foundation that you've established. Don't forget that it depends on the foundation whether the house is solid, or whether your children will take the wrong path. Good or bad news about your children affect mostly them, but ask yourself how much it affects you as a parent, and how much it can affect your work. No one can affect us like our children can, build up a high-quality relation with them and your life will have less turbulence.)

DON'T BRAG ABOUT BEING A GOOD HUSBAND OR WIFE, YOUR ACTIONS SPEAK FOR THEMSELVES

(There's nothing worse than a man bragging about being a good, faithful husband, and then spending more time with a mistress than with the wife and children together. Naturally, this open secret is known to the whole company and the company's partners. Although you might have the best qualities, you'll be profiled as a person who has an unstable marriage, who doesn't respect family values, who's ethics are very low. People will start having much different opinion of you. Therefore, Gentlemen, even if you really are this way, it's better to keep it to yourself and not to brag about it. This won't make it any better, but you will be more respected and less bad mouthed by your coworkers who would think that you are probably having big problems and that you don't want to talk about it, or that you are fighting to put things in the right places. It's not so nice, but that's life. I almost forgot, all this applies to the fair sex as well, there is no difference.)

DON'T JUDGE A MAN FROM HIS FAILURES, BUT FROM HIS EFFORTS TO CHANGE.

(One of the best examples is in my case: countless times, I heard different comments about my marriages, the nightlife, the rebellious nature, etc, but only few people realized the actual changes. During the period of failures and life changes, I was investing a lot into myself. Now, when the same people hear about the success that I achieved, while I was the subject of their badmouthing, they cannot get over it, they cannot believe that a young man can accomplish that much. Don't think that I'm blowing my own trumpet here, but I really suffered many insults, and lost many business deals precisely because of the people who were judging the book by its cover, and never took time to open it, and it's there that the truth is: I was making very big efforts to change. So, dear Gentlemen, don't judge other people through their failures or the town gossip, instead if you see they're making efforts to change things, compliment it and help them if you can, at least with your support, because those people won't forget that, and you'll always be able to count on them. In this way, you'll appear as man of vision, a flexible person who's always ready to support changes. That is a feature of great leaders.)

YOU'RE YOUR OWN BEST FRIEND AND WORST ENEMY.

(This is my favorite part because it may be the most important advice of this story. Believe me, everything that happens to you, good or bad, has its perpetrator, as I mentioned before, and it is you. This topic will be more explored in one of the next stories, but in this part, I would like to mention that in life you must rely solely on yourself and on your own results. This is a double-edged sword because you must build an efficient self-control system if you want to reach the heights. In most of the stories that I'm going to tell, you will realize that I was my own worst enemy, and when I understood that, I started to befriend myself. Does it sound a bit confusing? Let's sum up: the family and the business don't support your restlessness, your complexes, your fears, your omissions, etc, that's why it is necessary for you to built an efficient self-control system, and to always be your own best friend. That gives stability to your family, and at work you'll be considered as

someone who's stable, moderate, proactive, fair, social, etc, in other words, all that could put you in better position against those who explode over nothing, and spend the most of the day fighting with themselves.)

THERE ARE LIMITS IN GOING DOWN, BUT NOT IN SUCCEEDING.

(It's incredible how true this statement is, maybe some won't agree with me, but let me undeceive you. Maybe I'll sound like Marcus Aurelius in the famous piece *Meditations*, where the word death has an absolute predominance comparing to other words, but the reality is inevitable. Whether you're going down or you already hit the bottom in every sense, don't rush your death by making thoughtless moves. This is the period when you're the most vulnerable, so try using the last atoms of your strength for your comeback, because the limit in going down is premature death. Should Donald Trump have committed a suicide when he claimed bankruptcy, and when everybody said that he would never come back from the dead, of course in business terms? Of course, he didn't do it, and that's why today he's known as one of world's biggest gurus in change management. Despite our friend Donald, if you become too desperate and depressed, your end will be close, and this is the limit of going down. But what about succeeding? For succeeding sky is the limit, or better said—there are no limits. When you are a successful man and when the number of your successes is bigger than the number of your losses, then you give the impression of a fighter, a person not afraid of changes, person who turns problems into opportunities, or person whose motto is "there's no surrender". This is what is being appreciated; be an eternal fighter, everybody will know that you're not joking, and that you'll fight until the end. Those competitors are the most dangerous ones. I felt it on my own skin.)

LISTEN TO THE WISE PEOPLE'S ADVICES

(This is not really a big wisdom, but can you really repress your bad temper (I am a good example of having difficulties in repressing it) and admit that you're wrong? How many times did you spare some time, without a special reason, to have a conversation with an older person, whom you consider wise? Listening without considering and practicing what you learned, is like

riding a horse without a saddle: it's just the matter of time when you'll fall back on the ground. I'm mentioning this because many people don't know how to listen and make the wrong conclusions. The wisdom is gained by years, it's the way of living, and the ability to make the good decisions (this will be discussed separately). Sometimes, I hear that some of my decisions and actions are wise, but am I really a wise man? Of course not, I'm far from being a wise man, as far is the earth from the sun, but I carefully consider the advices from the people who have a lot of life experience, and I always try to get some benefit from those advices. A wise man is someone who had millions ups and downs, someone who tries passing you the life massages in the most efficient way, so that you avoid making the mistakes. How many times did I say to certain people "stop preaching me, I think I know how to do it", and then I got drowned in the drops. There are countless wise advices hidden in different places, in ordinary stories of even more ordinary people, in complex stories of magnificent people, in the books, etc. Don't reject those advices, dedicate some time to the wisdom; it is the only way that, you too one day, will give someone an advice, that you too will become wise, why not, that's also possible.)

Just to remind you on the advices from this story:

- **THE FAMILY MUST COME FIRST, NO COMPROMISES ACCEPTED.**

- **DON'T BRAG ABOUT BEING A GOOD PARENT, YOUR CHILDREN'S RESULTS WILL BEST PROVE IT.**

- **DON'T BRAG ABOUT BEING A GOOD HUSBAND OR WIFE, YOUR ACTIONS SPEAK FOR THEMSELVES**

- **DON'T JUDGE A MAN FROM HIS FAILURES, BUT FROM HIS EFFORTS TO CHANGE.**

- **YOU'RE YOUR OWN BEST FRIEND AND WORST ENEMY.**

- **THERE ARE LIMITS IN GOING DOWN, BUT NOT IN SUCCEEDING.**

- **LISTEN TO THE WISE PEOPLE'S ADVICES**

2

HOW MUCH TIME DO WE HAVE? WE HAVE NO TIME!

Oh my god, I've lost so much time! I know, many people say, "oh I wish I knew then (when I was young) what I know now, I would do miracles". It's incredible how a person can waste time and how much this can cost in the future, or better say COST, without the CAN. It really is that way.

I come from a rich family, but I wasn't born rich. During my childhood, my family developed a good business and made quite a fortune that fairly changed our way of living since the old days. Since I can remember I've heard stories about how difficult it was to earn the money, and even more difficult to keep it. Hoping that my thoughts will be read also outside the borders of my country, I need to describe where I was born and how I was growing up. That is necessary to be explained because it gives a special charm to the whole story.

I come from Serbia, a small country in the Balkans, which has spent its entire existence in wars, agitations, separations, slavery, poverty, etc (consequently, nothing pretty). I must also mention that the political agitations in the last thirty years put Serbia in an enviable place of corrupted countries, among the first ten in the whole world. What can I say; at least we have a lead at something. Even Columbia envies us. Naturally, my

country and my people have myriad qualities, but they're mostly repressed by bad things.

It's very simple; I've spent my youth in wars, manifestations, changes of political regimes, sanctions, poverty, misery, illnesses, everything was as it shouldn't be. While others were developing, we were having wars (luckily for us!) I'm mentioning all this so that you could have a better picture of the general conditions of the life in Serbia in the years 1990-2000. Therefore, dear Gentlemen, in all that chaos, I am trying for more than twenty-eight years to stay sane and to make life conditions more decent.

Most of you would ask, don't you come from a wealthy family, how come you didn't continue the family business, why do you have so many problems? I know, many people wondered, but I wouldn't be me, if one day I didn't leave home (because of the frequent quarrels with my father) and tried to change the world alone (what a stupid thing to do at that moment!). Again, my rebellious nature did its course. I wasn't away for a long time, but in the very short period, many things changed. Since the very young age I couldn't stand being defeated, however I never found victories being important (I take that from my father). Because of the bad economic situation that lasted over ten years (and it is not much better today), from 1990 until 2000, neither did my father's business go so well. Those were my teenage days and I wanted to have everything, which was not possible at all. My wishes were just overstepping the possibilities, and that made our family fights even more frequent. It was very hard for my parents; thank god, I didn't make them insane in that period.

Although, the whole situation had a positive side as well, I had this huge amount of energy that I didn't have where to spend (that's what I thought), except for making problems from time to time. All jokes aside, I really had this huge energy that I wanted to spend on useful things. My father complimented that, he use to say, "Son, now is the time to start working, this is the best age to learn how to become a boss (I was sixteen)". He spoke wisely. He spoke as man who was an orphan and who earned by himself everything that he owns. He spoke to his son, knowing how difficult it is to survive in this cruel word, especially in Serbia.

Unfortunately, I didn't hear what my father was saying, but I had an echo in my ears saying that that was the age to learn how to become a boss and constantly I wanted to have more. I had an opportunity to travel in developed countries (unlike 99% of Serbian kids) and to see how our country is poor and miserable. Besides, comparing to our country, I had a chance to realize that in those developed countries entirely opposite things

were appreciated. I had a chance to see that education is valued, that talent is valued, and that hard work pays out, etc. I thank God and my parents that I realized those things on time. While previously cited human values were appreciated in developed countries, at the same time, in my country, we valued crime, the education reached its lowest levels, if you were a know-it-all you could get hurt, the ones who were working hard didn't earn much money, so neither that was a smart thing to do. What can I say; it's hard to believe how geographically close we are to Great Britain, France or Italy, while in everything else we are at least a century apart.

Ok, since I've learned all this early enough, thank God, I realized that I HAVE NO TIME LEFT. I knew that it would take me much longer to make money doing a specific job in my country that it would taken me, doing the same job, in one of the developed countries, but I didn't have the possibility to choose. Believe me, my dear Friends, I wasn't picky at all: I did everything, all kind of jobs, I wasn't ashamed of doing anything, because I realized that comparing to people from developed counties, I was way beyond average.

"But where is your parents' fortune?" you would ask once again.

The fortune is there, as always, but once, in a big rage, I told my father that I didn't need anything from him and that I would do everything in life by myself, and much more than he did. Well, I decided to try it as well. I always had my parents' support, because they realized that I was on the right path, and that meant a lot to me. I had my own private business since the age of twenty, and simultaneously, I was finishing my studies. The more I worked the better were the relations with my family. I was doing two jobs at the same time while most of the people of my age were still wasting their time, having second thoughts about what they want, what kind of job they want to do. I was working in the manufacture of concrete blocks, I was building concrete blocks (where I permanently damaged my spine and made everlasting hand calluses), and when I finished that, I was working in my own fitness club, teaching the beginners, watching out someone doesn't get hurt, etc. You can't imagine all the working scenes: sacks of cement on my shoulders during the day and sets of weight during the afternoon. I was more than exhausted, but satisfied. I use to say that, until my thirties, I wish to open a bigger gym, and at least double up the number of exercise machines. I'm not in that business anymore, now without much trouble, I could open a big fitness center and workout alone in it, but unfortunately, I'm not any longer in that business. I also need to mention, that in that time, while I was doing the heaviest jobs and was earning not more than

two thousand dollars per month, I had over a million dollars in real estate, which my father was more than willing to hand me over (the fortune that I mentioned before). He was saying that it belonged to me, however, I didn't want to hear nothing about it, but that's another story.

Can you take any good advice from that story?

I'll try to help you. Here are some advices:

TIME IS WHAT YOU DON'T HAVE.

(It is very important that you realize this on time. If your conversations are full of sentences like, "Chill out, there's time, I'm still young", then you have a problem. Of course, if you are thirteen years old and you are reading this book, I don't suggest that you grab a sack of cement, but if you are a young manager or middle age person, then you probably get the message. Don't forget, rich people save time, while the poor save money. You don't have any time, and you must repeat it several times, every day. That way you will respect every minute of your time, as well as yourself, other people will know that you respect your time and will try not to waste it with excess comments. Every minute spent working is minute of building up your experiences. Try building up your experience early, because if you start boosting up your carrier and making experiences at the age of fifty, then your end will be more successful than your beginning; the end will be realized efficiently and quickly—that's what I meant.)

ACCEPT THE PRESENT.

(What's gone is gone; I am begging you, stop wasting your time by crying about the past. What will happen is uncertain, so the only real possibility that you have is to accept the present. I'm not telling you to stop dreaming and fantasizing; just don't fly too high, at least not in the beginning. For some time I was blaming my failures on the country that I'm living, then on my parents, then on the bad weather, then on the global warming, then on my failed relationships, then on my marriages, etc; so nothing intelligent. The easiest thing is to find quickly an excuse for the failure. In difficult situations, when things seem hard to carry out, people tend to pull back; they try to do another business, hoping it will be easier. I've managed to gather the strength and to play all or nothing; I accepted the country,

the parents, the bad weather, the global warming, the failed relationships, my famous marriages, I put everything on the side and started to clear the path to success. Even today, I like to take almost unsolvable business assignments, but only because I know that I will solve them and take the best of it for myself. Don't forget, besides the profits that you take from some job, you get something even more valuable—the experience, which will bring new jobs and more money. So face bravely your problems and accept the present, the bright future is coming for sure.)

ANALYZE THE PRAXIS OF THE BEST.

(This is very important, my dear Friends. I don't even know how my business would have turn out if I didn't have a chance to travel and live in the developed countries. If there's something that you don't know, it's not a shame to ask, don't be a wiseacre, and especially if it isn't about things from your expertise field; just ask the question politely and you'll get the answer. I use to think that I was so clever that I couldn't realize how much nonsense I was actually saying and how many times I made a fool of myself in front of the others. Don't do that, instead, try analyzing the praxis of the best, keep constantly learning, traveling and looking at the right things. We are so many on this planet, good business opportunities wait for you in every corner, all you have to do is get up from your comfortable armchair and have a walk, incredible things and people are hiding around the corner. All this will have a big impact on your job; the contact network that you will be building, will become way too big for your address book. Go ahead and do it!)

DON'T WASTE THE ENERGY.

(Directing your energy to the wrong things is like throwing away the money that you haven't earned yet. Sometimes, when I see crowded shops, I like to say that people are spending the money they don't have. That's right, most of us, ordinary people, live in the world of long-term/short-term financial obligations towards the new age loan sharks—the banks. However, what can we do when we like nice things, we like to eat, and the paycheck comes only the next month? Therefore, long live the credit cards and our dear banks. Why is it that I'm comparing energy with money? It's very simple,

24

I spent so much energy on wrong things and the only thing that it got me is a lesson (not to do it again), and in the meanwhile, if I'd been selling pens on the street, believe me, I'd earn a lot of money. Directing the energy properly brings much more than the job accomplishment. Directing the energy properly is the way of life, life with fewer drops. Don't waste the energy on irrelevant things, direct it on set goals, believe me, you'll be surprised how dry you and your surrounding will be—I'm talking about the drops, of course.

BE REBELLIOUS FOR THE RIGHT THINGS

(I always use to say that I'll make more money than my father did, and I always made a lot of noise about it. He was always smiling and saying, "Go ahead, I'd like to see that". Now, I know that he was glad that I was rebellious and stubborn, but for the right thing. Probably he wouldn't be smiling if I'd been saying that I was going to be a bigger drug dealer than Pablo Escobar, but since my goals were set for the right things, he was satisfied and always very supporting. You cannot believe how difficult it would have been for me if I didn't have my parents' support. Certainly, I wouldn't be where I am now; I would have achieved much less. So, feel free to make noise about the right things, be rebellious and stubborn for something good, because being rebellious when it's about something good is like directing the energy properly and spending time rationally, and that is enough for starting your business. You give the impression of a dynamic person with a set goal; these persons are not to joke with. I'm not to joke with, and what about you?)

Just to remind you on the advices from this story:

- **TIME IS WHAT YOU DON'T HAVE**

- **ACCEPT THE PRESENT**

- **ANALYZE THE PRAXIS OF THE BEST**

- **DON'T WASTE THE ENERGY**

- **BE REBELLIOUS FOR THE RIGHT THINGS**

3

DO YOU LOOK LIKE A SEX BOMB?

In my house, if you don't throw away food after every meal, it means it wasn't enough of it (very good philosophy for throwing away the money and gaining extra weight). Imagine every meal, on the table enough food to feed ten people, while there is only five of us. I've already told you that my father was an orphan and that he was always dreaming about the food, so the table always had to have abundance of food, after all, he's the man of the house.

I'm mentioning all that because I spent all my childhood looking fat like a pig, right until the high school. I was accepted in the police school, which was a boarding school so I managed, doing workouts, to get my shape. When I realized that with a right nutrition and workouts I could look like a sex bomb (I'm saying this on purpose because of the coming story), you could not believe what I did with myself. With time, no one was recognizing me, but neither this magnificent period of my life lasted long. Once again, my rebellious nature took its course and under various circumstances, I hurt myself during the workout. Back then, I was working-out twice a day, but I overdid it on the second workout, I wanted to wreak my anger, my failures and my losses on the boxing bag

and working-out equipment. I overdid it to the point that I had to change my residence and spend three months in hospital.

The injury was heavy, the operation was complicated, the doctors struggled for my life, but luckily, at the end, the patient is writing the book. The recovery took more than a year, and my six-pack abs turned into the barrel. I've put more than 27 kilos and I looked like a balloon. I couldn't wait to recover completely and get back my old weight. This time I was working-out much smarter, I was leaving my problems in the locker room, while my workouts became carefully planned and there was no exaggeration. For a long time I had a trauma from being injured and it took me long to completely let loose during the workouts. Imagine working out twice a day, being crazy about it, and then suddenly you lose all that for a year, while your looks go from normal to super fat. Therefore, my Friends, a disaster, but life goes on.

People who know me, know that I workout on regular bases, with occasional pauses, of course, but I try to keep in the shape, first for the health reasons, and then for the looks. Of course, no one wants to be a balloon if he can look like a sex bomb (I don't know why, but I love this expression). Many of you will say that workout injuries are something that could happen to everyone and there's nothing strange about them. Dear Gentlemen, most of the workout injuries are products of our unstable minds, and sometimes, they can even be fatal.

Besides, I was also practicing judo and wrestling. I was participating in many wrestling competitions, and certainly, there are strong possibilities to get hurt practicing this sport, but difficult injuries, like mine was, usually come as consequences of bad concentration, then from anything else. Besides wrestling, I was also practicing bodybuilding, which I continue even today, much more than judo and wrestling. If once you are a fighter, you'll always be a fighter. If once you look like a sex bomb, you'll always want to look like a sex bomb. Don't tell me that you wouldn't want to look drop dead gorgeous. This is quite normal, everyone likes to look good, but you need to be constantly working on yourself, you need to make it a way of living.

So, make a strip show in front of the mirror and try to be critical on yourself. Don't forget, the girl cannot be a little pregnant, she's pregnant or she's not, it's the same in this case, you look like a sex bomb or you don't.

Can you take any good advices from this story?

I'll try to help you. Here are some advices:

EAT TO LIVE; DON'T LIVE TO EAT.

(This is very important, I'm not going to give you advices about what you should eat, I'm far from being a nutritionist, but I know one thing: enjoy food as much as it is necessary for your organism to function and nothing more than that. If you follow this philosophy, you will never have problems with extra kilos. Does the overweight make you feel less self-confident, or should I say not confident at all? Does it affect your work in any way? I'll let you answer to that alone.)

WORK ON YOUR DISCIPLINE.

(The discipline is very important, it is crucial during the meals, during the workouts but also in business. If you don't have discipline during your meals, you will have extra weight, which will make you nervous and unsatisfied, which can lead you to get injured during the workout, and the injury will make such a big flood of drops, that you'll need a miracle to go back where you were. Does this have to do anything with work? Could you afford, due to the lack of discipline, to be absent for one year from the work, and expect that everything would be the same when you come back? I'll let you answer to that alone.)

WORK ON YOURSELF.

(You have to be working-out constantly. You must practice any kind of sports; I don't mean playing dominoes or chess, but a real physical training. You'll look better, you'll be healthier, your concentration will be on high levels, and the business results won't be questioned.)

YOU SHOULD LOOK LIKE A SEX BOMB.

(Of course, this whole story about the sex bomb could sound a bit exaggerated, pretentious, etc, but please, please, I'm begging you, don't lie to yourself and to me by saying that you don't want to look like Brad Pitt or Angelina Jolie. It's normal, but it takes many sacrifices and continuous work. Everyone at work and outside of it will notice that you've been

working out, you'll become more pleasant to the eye (especially if you are a woman), you will be more self-satisfied and the business results will be magnificent. Your appearance, of course, is really, really far from being crucial for making the business deals, but still, it says a lot about the person; if you have in front of you a person who takes care about his/her looks, it can only be a big plus and never something negative. When I see a person who doesn't take care of his/her appearance, who's so sloppy that you could see it with your bare eyes, I always say, "My God, how will this person treat us in business, when he's treating himself like this?" You should never allow this to happen; always give the impression of a tidy person who takes care of himself/herself. If I were to judge you, this would already give you a huge plus.)

BE SELF-CRITICAL.

(We all have our differences, we really do. You have to be self-critical and set your own standards. I'm not talking about exaggerating, but you cannot stand in front of the mirror kicking your belly with your knees, and say: I don't look that bad. Be reasonable in criticizing your appearance, behaviors, etc, but try to be self-critical, because, trust me, no one is perfect, but we all try be close to the perfection. That's why you should admit when you've made a mistake, admit when you're fat, admit that you're average in your job, but please, you have to mean it as well. Why do I say all this? You know how women always say that they have extra weight, even when they don't, that is natural, because they like to hear that they look good. Believe me, it's the same thing with the men, they just don't want to admit it. You must be honest, primarily to yourself, don't admit some things just to please your company or to finish faster some conversation. Admit everything from the heart, be self-critical for yourself, and not for the others, they will respect you more.)

Just to remind you on the advices from this story:

- **EAT TO LIVE; DON'T LIVE TO EAT**

- **WORK ON YOUR DISCIPLINE**

- **WORK ON YOURSELF**

- **YOU SHOULD LOOK LIKE A SEX BOMB**

- **BE SELF-CRITICAL**

4

DON'T JUDGE THE BOOK
BY ITS COVER

I can be unbelievably brutal when I see an almost perfect company affected by cancer. There's no help to that, but it's like with people who have cancer, if we act in an early stadium, maybe we can stop the spreading of the disease. It's the same thing when we talk about the companies.

There are some jobs that I really don't like doing, and I always like to transfer them to someone else (once a manager, always a manager); especially when I have to go to the store, in any kind of shopping, to pour out gas or to take money from the bank. I really cannot explain it, but in these moments, it feels like a volcanic eruption happening inside me, because it's something that really has to be done, but I always feel that I'm wasting a lot of time that I don't have (remember the story about not having time).

Anyway, I always try to transfer those obligations to others, but there's another obligation that probably annoys me the most, and that is going to the tire-repairing specialist. Since I have several cars and I don't really care which one I'll drive to work, usually I notice some defaults on the car, caused by the lack of attention of the previous driver (my father, my wife, or the employed driver). When this default involves the tire repairmen, you

better not be close by, but my dear Gentlemen, not because I have to go where I don't like to, but because of the drop effect (an unplanned situation ruins your day, and if you're lucky, just that one day), cause the day in question finished up completely differently than I'd planned.

It was late November, very cold outside, and my car was begging for a tire repair specialist. There was a problem with the tire pressure and the summer tires needed to be changed into the winter ones (which, of course, I didn't know). I called at work and explained what was happening, to which they told me that, anyway they were planning, but imagine, WERE PLANNING, to go to check the tires and change them as well. There was no use in wasting my voice on the phone, I've learned long time a go that yelling doesn't make me right, and it's also much more effective to rub someone's nose with normal tone of voice (still water runs deep).

I told them to make a payment for the new tires and the services to that company, and I will go to finish that job, since it is on my way to work. If I knew what I was about to experience, I would take the taxi. The company that was supposed to change the tires was advertised on every radio station, on every billboard, there were lines of cars waiting in front of their garage, and my employees, of course, chose them, as a logical choice. I arrived in front of the company that was positioned on a very good location for that kind of activity, the administration building and the warehouse were built in highest standards, so the first impression was, "WOW, what a sophisticated company!" However, this was only the cover of the book; here is what the content was.

Actually, I was already starting to drown slowly in the drops, what a horror! When I said what company I was coming from, the information officer told me that he was sorry but he didn't have the time to make the invoice so that we could make the payment. The invoice was already issued by his colleague, and we already put down the payments, but he didn't even know about it. Completely shocked, holding my bank statement in his hand, he informs me what to do next. Here's where the comedy starts. He said, " . . . Now, you must go to our warehouse, there, they will put a stamp on your invoice and give you the tires; and you will get to the warehouse by passing by the garage where the tires are being installed, then turn left and after that you'll probably see around there the door of the warehouse."

I started to laugh. My cell phone was full of missed calls and text messages; my secretary was drowning in the drops because of my drops, because she couldn't explain where the General Manager was at that moment; of course, she couldn't say that I was in the search of tire warehouse, and

that the outcome of this search was unknown. After the administration clerk gave me such a detailed description of my future destination, in other words, the warehouse, I headed off to it, and on my way, I had to ask three more employees where the warehouse was. Of course, no need to mention how polite they were: they were barely opening their mouths, while some of them were just showing the direction with their hand. For a moment, I thought I was on Candid Camera.

In the warehouse, I had to wait for 15 minutes for the clerk to check if I really made the payment for the tires, and after a detailed check up, he finally brought himself to put the stamp. Afterwards, he didn't say anything, so I had to conclude that probably, I had to go back to the garage for the installment of the tires. The garage employees were passing by me, as if I wasn't there; I thought that in any moment someone was going to give me some wrench and say, "What are you waiting for? Grab this and do something useful". I couldn't wait any longer, so I asked with high tone of voice, "Excuse me who works here on the admission?" A young guy with a snotty nose came and said, "Gimme that papers to see what it is." I mean, it was as if I was at the investigation court and not at the tire repairman.

I was chocking in agony and laughter.

Around me, there were some other customers, who were sharing my destiny, but this is Serbia, there's no way you would dare to reproach something to persons who are fixing your car, at risk to get the job badly done, oh yes, long live the anarchy! In the next place, the young man that I mentioned before, put the stamp on the forth paper and told me that I had to go back to the initial counter, for them to put another stamp. I answered politely: "But Sir, ("*Snotty, wipe your nose at least*", I didn't say that), I was already there before, are you certain that I have to go back there?" I got a short answer (with a dull look in the eyes), "Yes". Then the young man asked, "But where are your tires? Which ones are yours?" I was completely shocked; he was walking around the garage looking for the tires that have been brought from the warehouse, and when he found them, with his finger, he showed me where they were. Oh, Serbia, my motherland, what is going on here?

I went again to the counter, I waited 25 minutes (I counted, because every minute was precious to me), I got the famous stamp, and the clerk (a woman this time) told me that I could go now again to the garage to give them the stamped paper and my tires will be installed. Once again, I was in the garage, the young man said briefly, "We are already installing your tires; I don't need that, you must wait, it won't be long." The next 30

minutes I was waiting for the job to be done; incidentally, there were some survey questionnaires lying on the table next to which I was waiting. They were meant for the customers to valuate (if they wished) the work of the company and give some suggestions.

You cannot imagine how it made me feel: it was as if I saw water in the middle of the desert! It didn't matter if it was going to be read by the Marketing or the PR Manager of the company, but hoping that they will read it, I filled up the complete survey, as for the part meant for the suggestions, it didn't have enough lines for me.

I'm not going to write what I recommended to a company affected by cancer; instead, before the advices from this story, I want to say only one thing: never, ever judge a book by its cover; it's an illusion that can cost you a lot. Thank god, it hadn't cost me much that day, and the lesson I learned is much more valuable than the lost time.

Can you take any good advices from this story?

I'll try to help you. Here are some advices:

BE PERFECT IN THE JOBS YOU HATE.

(The previous story made you see the things that I really don't like doing, and how negligent I was in committing to things that could have a big influence on my life. You should always do first the things that you find the most difficult, the most complicated or that you really don't like doing; the everyday things, like those things that I don't like doing, you must do them perfectly, because small things bring out big problems. It goes the same when doing business or at your work place. It's natural that you don't like, for example communicating with some people, but try to give your best when doing things that you don't like, because, in other things, that really suit you, you will be brilliant.)

DON'T SHARE YOUR THINGS WITH ANYONE.

(This applies only to the personal things that are necessary for accomplishing efficiently everyday obligations. It's incredible how your day can be deranged from the things like a lack of gasoline, a visit to the tire repair specialist, an accidently infiltrated virus in your laptop by your children, a page accidently thorn from your notebook by your wife who was writing

down a pie recipe, and so on. That's why is necessary not to share those things with anyone, believe me, it will cost you a lot.)

DON'T JUDGE THE BOOK BY ITS COVER.

(So, when everything seems perfect on the outside, don't expect to be the same on the inside. There is a number of case studies that suggest being careful in the situations of that kind. I like to divide the *Don't Judge the Book by Its Cover* situation in the following way: 1) Instant disappointment (my case with the tires) and 2) Sudden disappointment (these disappointments are the most dangerous ones, and they're usually hiding in the companies that are seemingly perfect. Yes, this is the worst possible situation that could happen to you. Imagine negotiating with a company that's perfect, but too good to be true, that's a sign to stop and think it over, because it's impossible to be that way, and there are always different motives hiding behind those companies.) No matter how good the proposal is, always ask yourself, "How can it be true?" I'm assuring you it's not. I had situations like this, but fortunately, my intuition helped me realize exactly the same thing: this is too good to be true, even the biggest corporations are not that good, there's something smelling here. I was right, the company I was supposed to be doing business with, was perfect, and that perfectness was a mask for frauds worth millions. That company doesn't exist anymore, it has huge debts, and the money is impossible to be tracked. The similar example was explained in the book called *Swim with the Sharks without Being Eaten Alive* by Harvey McKay—must read it, good examples and advices are never enough.

BE PATIENT IN TENSE SITUATIONS.

(I know that it's hard and that you, probably, just like I did, exploded and yelled many times on your employee or on some tire repair worker or so, but that's a mistake. Don't forget, still water runs deep. Calmly pronounced words affect the most, because they make you sound like you don't care about anyone's stupidity or incompetence, and that you know what you are talking about, when it comes to your job and things that you want. I admit, there were moments at that tire repair shop, when I wanted to start shouting, but it would just made everyone say, "Look at

that lunatic screaming, what an impolite person". For the start, I filled up the questionnaire form, but considering the kind of company they are, I seriously doubt anyone is going to read it. It's important that you stay calm, your life goals are not directed to tire repair specialists and their warehouse, but to much more important things, so be smart and refrain yourself. I get use to say: the easiest thing is to be a fool, yes a real fool, you just throw a brick on your neighbor's window and your goal is achieved, instead try acting like a normal human being, and you'll realize it's much more difficult, but also a much wiser solution. Patience is a much-valued virtue that needs to be practiced; it could help you a lot in your job, because hasty moves are usually thoughtless as well. Those are all products of the impatience, so please, for the start, your friend—the author, is begging you, practice your patience, there's no better tool for dealing with the problems in these crazy times.)

BECOME A CLIENT IN YOUR OWN COMPANY.

(If I would tell my tire repair adventure to the owner of that shop, he would probably be completely shocked. If Mr. Owner would say that it is not true, then Gentlemen, the problem would be more than obvious and we would find the real cause. Anyway, the vital part of the company, the employees, is affected by the cancer; especially those employees who are at the first line of defense, but I'm not the one who should be noticing, that's the owner's job. It is necessary that you occasionally become a customer or a client in your own company; it is the best way to understand the defaults. This is a good recipe, I did a similar thing at one of my construction sites and I got some unbelievable information. Don't forget, the most important resource is the human resource; it's the basis of your company. If the cancer affects the bases, an urgent reform and restructure are necessary, because the company is slowly dying, while you think it's flourishing, all because you don't see further than your comfortable chair and your oak table. My dear Friends, don't be lazy, whether you are the owner, a head of department, or a worker, always put yourself in the opposite position, make the length and breadth tour of your company and you will see where you stand, or where you don't, and you would like to be.

KEEP IMPROVING YOURSELF FOREVER.

(It is very important that you keep up with the times, no matter what your position in the company is. If you keep standing in one place, don't forget that the rest of the world is moving in an incredible speed. The man who's the owner of the tire repair company affected by cancer has serious problems, and he's not even aware of them. It seems that he has reached the first level of business development and he encountered an obstacle called WHAT NEXT. However, he's not even aware of that. I always use to say, if there's something that you don't know, well just ask, it's not shameful to ask. A company has to follow the trends and be an organization that is learning and constantly improving. The competition never rests and is always developing, so you must try to improve yourself in every possible way, it's the only way to survive and not to live up the destiny of that poor tire repair specialist, who, in my opinion, won't stay there much longer.

Just to remind you on the advices from this story:

- **BE PERFECT IN THE JOBS YOU HATE.**

- **DON'T SHARE YOUR THINGS WITH ANYONE.**

- **DON'T JUDGE THE BOOK BY ITS COVER.**

- **BE PATIENT IN TENSE SITUATIONS.**

- **BECOME A CLIENT IN YOUR OWN COMPANY.**

- **KEEP IMPROVING YOURSELF FOREVER.**

5

COURAGE IS THE MAGIC CRAZINESS

Many authors of books in the field of psychology, as well as many management consultants, describe courage as a special virtue of the humankind. Every person is unique, we all function in a specific, individual way in this hell. Many things shouldn't be generalized; but is it possible to generalize the people's courage, can we say that only successful people are brave, and the unsuccessful are cowards? Mark McCormack, in the book entitled *What They Don't Teach You at Harvard Business School*, speaks about this phenomenon. He explains his early beginnings and describes how much strength it took him to leave the job that he was doing, and to start his own business (I strongly recommend that you read it).

I don't know why, but in all my life experience (which is not very long since I'm only 28), I was trying to balance the opportunities that I was getting. I never got in problems out of caprice or anger (ok, maybe once or twice, when I was very young, every man has that phase) because I knew it was going to drag along even bigger problems. My dear Serbia is quite an insecure place to live; through history, we killed ourselves most of our leaders and kings, which puts us—the average citizens, in the same pot with the sparrows or eventually the street dogs, when it comes to our own

life security. I was always advised by my parents (especially because of my rebellious nature) to stay aside and not to fight other people's battles. That's true, it bothers me a lot to see injustice, it feels like a volcanic eruption inside me and I really have hard time dealing with it.

To be able to keep the life style that I have, I always tried to be above the everyday problems. Trust me, in my life I had a chance to meet different people, from my fellow professors to hardcore criminals, simply because I was in that kind of circles (everybody was in that kind of circles in Serbia, during the economical embargo and the war, in the period from 1990-2000). At the end, when I draw the line, I'm glad that I had a chance to meet people from the both worlds. I usually like to say that if you want to survive in Serbia (and that goes for the rest of the world as well), you must learn how to swim. What I'm about to say is not even an open secret anymore, the crime is that much involved in the Serbian economy that it is not even interesting anymore, it's extremely funny, but you either swim or drown yourself, there's no third option. I explained all this so people outside the borders of this country could get the picture of the conditions in Serbia. Currently, big democratic changes are being implementing, but there's a long way to go before the situation gets completely fixed.

In this story, I'm describing the courage as a magic craziness. I think that we are all courageous, but not in every situation, some are courageous enough to enter the tigers' cage, but are scared to swim far from the shore, etc. That's why there are many kinds of courage, and I would generalize like follow: all the people are brave, but not for the same things.

The type of courage I respect the most is the one directed to the family and to the improvement of the standard of living. Dear Gentlemen, it is very difficult to succeed in my country, in five years I already expect to have some kind of psychiatric diagnosis, because what offends me the most, as a human being, is insolence and stupidity. I've already mentioned that I started my own business very early in life, but that lasted only for a while. After I've graduated, I had opportunities to work for many companies but we never could agree about the working conditions.

Why is it so?

Believe me, I understand those people, my conditions were horrible, no one could agree to that. However, those were my requests: take it or leave it. I had energy for three people, I knew that, but they didn't. That's why I decided to start a more serious business that involved big money investment and knowledge. I had an old house on a good location that

was perfect for constructing a residential building, but because of some property issues, my location was problematic. I had a co-owner on the location, who didn't want to move out. I won't get into the details; I'll just explain the most important parts. For constructing that kind of premises, it takes more than half million dollars, and then I also needed money for the design of the construction project, for the government taxes, etc; but believe it or not, I was completely broke. It was important that I realized what the problem was, and it couldn't wait any longer to solve it. I had the house and the lot, and at the same time, I didn't; a profit ready right in my hands, and at the same moment, so very far, like the earth from the sun. The situation in the country was never worse, there was no money at all, crime and usury were flourishing and newly graduated managers didn't even have enough to pay for a taxi. That was the very image of my beloved city and country.

I said to my father that I didn't want to work for others, and that I want to spend all my energy on myself. I was in a very difficult situation, my first daughter was almost two years old back then, and I was already divorced for the second time. (Just to get the whole picture of my situation at the time). I decided to go all for nothing. I called my lawyer and made an appointment. I borrowed from one friend 50 dollars, because I didn't have enough money to get to my lawyer's, to whom I explained my extremely good plan to earn millions. During the meeting, I asked the lawyer to do all that was in his power to start the construction and to try to get the consent of the co-owner of the lot. The lawyer said that the consent won't be a problem, but I had to move out the co-owner before the registration of the building. As if I was on drugs, I said, "Let me worry about that, I'll take care of it; you just make sure that I can start the construction". He agreed, and casually asked if I've secured the money for the beginning of the construction, to which I said that, also that was my problem, and that I'll take care of it on time. When I left his office, I couldn't catch my breath; after all, I was only 23 years old and I was showing off like I was at least Donald Trump.

Time came to find the money.

It was a nightmare, I didn't sleep for three days, but I found a solution. I decided to borrow the money, not the whole sum, just enough to start the construction, to make it until the ground floor. Days were passing by, I knocked on many doors, but I failed to get a positive response. In the meanwhile, the lawyer called to inform me that everything was ok, and he said that I could start the construction. When I heard that, I completely

lost my sleep. I had no choice but to go to usurers to borrow the money. That was the first time in my life that I asked my father to give me one of the flats so I could put it as collateral for the loan. He was more than furious, he didn't like my idea, and he didn't like me starting a business that I didn't know so well (I use to do some interior renovation jobs with a small team during my studies, that was the only experience that I had in constructing). I didn't want to hear anything about it, I asked him to have faith in me, and if he didn't want to, I'd never speak to him again (God, I hope one of my children won't turn up like this!). I refused to take the money from my father; all I wanted is for him to let me put one of the flats as collateral.

At the end, he accepted but only if he was also involved in the constructing, as my advisor and help (I accepted instantly). You cannot believe how ugly it is to take the money from the usurers, but that money taking, is what gave me an extra strength to fight even more, so never again I will have to come back to that place where I signed the contract with the loan sharks.

The construction started, I barely got to the ground floor and the crises started again; the workers wanted to continue and I didn't have the money to go on. Sleepless nights again, where to find the money now, there was only to pawn a kidney (I was only thinking aloud). The agony lasted for three days; desperate, I was analyzing my actions, and thinking of how much I was putting at stake, and suddenly my father called. He said that he had a client who wanted to buy an apartment under construction. I was overwhelmed with joy, and to make things even better, the sale was completed. The construction continued and wherever I could, I tried to sell apartments in the same way. In less than a month, I sold four flats; afterwards, everything started to go upwards.

To make a long story short, I finished the building on time. I moved and paid out well the co-owner, registered the building, paid the protection rackets to everyone who asked, and even to those who didn't (sometimes I think that the Serb is born with a corruption gene; actually nowhere else I saw corruption like in Serbia, with few exceptions and myself, really nowhere, but that's life as well), and the loan sharks were respected. I made big money (everything was big for me at that moment), but the most important was that my father gained huge faith in me. He pronounced the following words, "I am crazy, but you are even crazier, I don't know where you found the courage to start this craziness, you did it more by good luck than by good judgment, but fortune favors the bold".

Construction is one of the prime activities of my company, now I'm already making the fifth building, and I'm planning to make five more until the age of 35. By now, most of you probably think that I'm exaggerating. Oh yes, I know, but if you've made a bet that I wouldn't build up my first building, you'd surely lose. It's better not to make bets with me; I always say that one should never quit, and that one should always, in every situation, no matter how difficult it gets, act courageously. My dear Friends, "courage is the magic craziness".

Can you take any good advices from this story?

I'll try to help you. Here are some advices:

EVERYBODY IS COURAGEOUS AND EVERBODY IS FEARFUL

(Dear Friends, watch up everyone around you. In this crazy world, you never know how willing anyone of us is to succeed. I said this on purpose, and it's really like this, everybody is courageous and everybody is fearful. You probably think of yourself as a brave person, but how many times did it happen that you caught yourself in a situation and said, "I absolutely can't do it, I'm a coward"? Everyone said it at least once in a lifetime. Always have in mind the title of this advice, because it doesn't write on anyone's face if they're brave or not, and in most cases, people usually like to follow the example of others. This is where the biggest trap is hidden. Maybe at the beginning I wasn't ready to face some things, now though, those same things are my favorite. Can you imagine the surprise in people eyes when they see that I'm handling pretty well some problems (and I used to have difficulties solving them in the past), and that I am determined and brave, to the point that I won't give up even under the greatest pressure? Don't let others' business example be your guide for the negotiations, or for reaching the agreement, people are constantly changing, for better and for worse, which is why it is crucial that, at the time, you make a good assessment of the situation and decide what would be the best way to deal with it. Don't forget, we might be cowards for some things, but in certain moments the fear can make us react in a way that can change the whole situation, here is the surprise that you weren't ready for. That's why you should be ready for the unexpected, without underestimating or hesitating, concentrate to the maximum—and just go for it!)

BE ABOVE THE PROBLEMS.

(Imagine me, going mad from the problems before starting the construction of my first building. I thought I was losing my mind, I was drowning in the flow of drops and it seemed like there was no way out. I was mismanaging the problems, which created even more problems. You have to be beyond the problems. You are probably going to ask yourself, how can I be above the problems when they press me all over, and when I don't see the way out? Don't forget what I'm about to say, there is always a way out of the problem, the only question is how much is that way out going to cost. Sometimes you give a dollar to get a job and three to get out of that job. No matter what kind of problem you face, you have to take it like a challenge, not like a tragedy. You cannot imagine how self-pitiful I was, and how much I was annoying the others with my problems. In those moments, besides your absence, you show something much worse—your weakness. You are not able to manage efficiently your problems, and you are becoming more and more vulnerable, although you know that a wounded animal cannot survive long in the jungle, and it's the first to be attacked by the jackals. When you leave the impression of being beyond the problems (regardless the volcanic eruptions happening daily in your head and body), I repeat, people see you as a tough rival, that knows how to swim with big fish, and is not afraid to do it. Problems are opportunities; by solving one big problem (in this case I built a building when it seemed like mission impossible) I became a different man. Now I see problems as opportunities, and it gives me a great pleasure dealing with much more difficult things, than it was in the case of my story of the first building. Weight your decisions wisely, only then you'll be able to manage the problems, and won't let them manage you.)

LEARN HOW TO SWIM

(If you say that never in your life, you've met a person from the other side of the law, then I must tell you that you've missed a lot, but that's not a problem, you can come to Serbia and it will be solved. I had a chance to meet, acquaint, and do business with people from the other side of the law. Believe me, it's nothing special, only in the begging of their carriers they were doing things the easy way, and now they're pretending to be businesspersons. Serbia is full of people like that. I know that everywhere

in the world, there are these kinds of people, but here their concentration is extremely high. Simply everyone who's involved in any kind of serious business in my country will eventually, encounter the tough guys. Nevertheless, that's a different story, for now I'll just tell you that life brings us big temptations, and sometimes there are no other options. I've entered a completely new world and I came to know jackals of different strength. If I confronted the first one, I'd probably be writing this book from behind the bars, and it would have a slightly different content, but I knew I had to swim, and even more important, I had to maintain the balance constantly. No matter if you are in Serbia or in the United States, sharks are everywhere, you must learn to swim with them, or otherwise, it's simple, you're not in the business.)

DON'T DEFY DESTINY, BUT TRY TO TAKE THINGS IN YOUR OWN HANDS

(Dear Gentlemen, don't suppress the volcano that wants to explode inside you, stop persistently trying to prevent it. Sometimes, it's enough to open your eyes to be able to see. Don't defy the destiny; instead let yourself go. I understand this could have enormous consequences, but you cannot withhold that discovery from yourself. This story makes you see that, despite all the trouble and problems, I have succeeded to accomplish my goal, which made me realize that I can carry even the biggest problems on my back. Let the volcano explode, you probably won't be sleeping, probably you'll be extremely nervous, probably you'll be cursing yourself for letting that happen; but when it all gets over, you'll feel invincible, and that is such a perfect feeling.)

BE STEP BEFORE ALL THE OTHERS.

(I've put on a nice little act pretending to be step before all the others, as you could see from this story. I wasn't step before the others, but I was just acting as if I was. Don't do that, it doesn't work every time. Analyze your possibilities carefully, but always try having an ace in your sleeve. What does it mean in a business sense? It means that you must always have a back-up version for the job that you've started. Don't ever tolerate blackmailing, because no one is irreplaceable. For each of us there's an adequate, if

not even better, replacement, but you must plan this replacement very carefully, so it could react on time when you need it. A late engagement of the replacement can cost you a lot, and the drop effect is disastrous in that case. Make sure you have good replacements, and that will make you step before all the others, and then let them try to mess with you.)

CRAZINESS IS JUSTIFIED FOR POSITIVE THINGS

(I think the way that I've accomplished my first big construction project gives a lot of material for diagnosing me as mentally deranged person. There were some details that I hadn't mention, but if you were present, you would be assured that there's something wrong with me. That's true, there was something wrong about me, I wanted more, and in this country, that was the only way to achieve it. Of course, I didn't borrow money from the usurers and then went to casino, that equals a suicide, but the money was borrowed for a positive thing. I knew I was doing a crazy thing, but it was for the positive cause. That's why I was pushing it so much, that's why I succeeded. Craziness is justified only for positive things.)

FORTUNE FAVORS THE BOLD.

(You've seen the epilogue at the end of the story, but you've also seen the way it all happened. In a certain moment, when life offers you an opportunity, you simply must take the risk. Gather your guts and make the step, but not a step behind, don't pull back, make a step forward even if it seems to be leading to the abyss. If it's the step for the right thing, you don't have to be afraid of the abyss, the earth under your feet might be invisible, but you'll still be walking and you will touch the solid ground again. The first time is like this, fortune favors the bold, just go ahead and do it!)

Just to remind you on the advices from this story:

- **EVERYBODY IS COURAGEOUS AND EVERBODY IS FEARFUL**

- **BE ABOVE THE PROBLEMS.**

- LEARN HOW TO SWIM

- DON'T DEFY DESTINY, BUT TRY TO TAKE THINGS IN YOUR OWN HANDS

- BE STEP BEFORE ALL THE OTHERS.

- CRAZINESS IS JUSTIFIED FOR POSITIVE THINGS

- FORTUNE FAVORS THE BOLD.

6

WATCH OUT GUYS, THE WOMEN'S ERA IS COMING, WE'LL EAT YOU UP ALIVE

Incredibly enough, we, guys always think that we are superior to women in business and that under no circumstances women should be put in top responsible positions, in private or in public sector (try saying that to Angela Merkel or Hilary Clinton). For a moment, let's leave the stereotypes behind, and try to realize the true essence of the problem. Men, the stronger sex (I'm one of the representative as well), are the real problem. They like to think that they are born to be on the strongest positions, no matter the type of activity, except in the cases of pregnancy and around the kitchen.

Of course, one should never question the role of the women concerning the pregnancy or them being the pillars of the family, we could never even imagine ourselves in that role. All those who say they could do it, are simply liars; they wouldn't last even for one day, or a minute on the birth table.

The global business tendencies show an increasing presence of the women in executive positions, but still, the number is less then low when compared to men. This story describes how we, men are far from being

perfect, and that women are equal opponents, if not even the more capable ones.

Every woman is special in her own way; all more frequent are the examples of women whose charisma and acuteness are captivating to the point that leave even the biggest leaders breathless. Yes, dear Gentlemen, you must admit that women are like miracles. Me, for example, I used to think that we, men are much superior to women (when it comes to business), but all the years of experience with doing business with the opposite sex, show that I was wrong. The Western women and women from the developed countries have much more freedom, than the women from the Balkan countries do. It is not a question of religion, it's the customs and the way of living that put the woman in less favorable position, which doesn't let them express their talents. It also has a very big influence on the valuation system at Balkan women, but neither that is going to last forever. I simply adore women (that's not the reason I had three marriages), I realized that their grace, their tenderness but also their endurance at the same time, affect the male sex to the point that we must give in, and start working shoulder to shoulder.

A number of times, in my work history, I had business deals with the fair sex, so it is very hard for me to choose one special story, except for the one that made me see the women with different eyes. Like every young jackal, whenever I spot an attractive prey (a woman), it makes my mouth water. Women use to serve me for one use only (probably many used me in the same way, too, so everyone was happy), and I didn't have many chances to do some serious business with a member of the fair sex. Not until the day when a certain lady answered the ad for renting the business premises owned by my company, she wanted to rent that space for her company. One of my employees showed that woman the premises, she liked them and then she insisted on meeting with the owner to arrange the details. I usually don't do that, I prefer to leave it to one of the managers and the company lawyer, but for some unknown reasons, I decided actually to do it this time.

A very attractive girl entered the door. She was not more than thirty years old, blond hair, dressed professionally (without obvious slits and unbuttoned shirts), perfectly tailored clothes were emphasizing her perfectly shaped figure (which showed that she was working out and that she was taking care of herself). Her sexuality was so radiant that it couldn't leave anyone indifferent, while the self-confident look in her eyes said that she was a real fire. My first thought was, "Where were you all my life?" I smelled

the prey, only, my dear Gentlemen, I didn't eat up, and I remained hungry, but satisfied. The conversation was going in the right direction, not even for a moment I let her know that I'd be more than happy to lock up the office so we could expand our views, and I'd be lying if I say that I haven't thought about it (every man would think about it, every single man). She saw my (so-called) indifference and total commitment to work. Since my knowledge of the business field that I'm involved is very wide, several times I tried to appear smart and show off my superiority, but with no apparent success. This young lady had quite a big knowledge in several business fields, to the point that I wanted her for my own company, and I can tell you, during that meeting my feelings were mixed with jealousy and fear. I was thinking to myself, "thank god this girl is not my enemy". Naturally, I know where my limits in business are, so I cannot imagine who could show up and make me go against my personality and my own boundaries. That was also the case here. That gave me a negotiation advantage since the young lady really liked the premises, but that advantage was only in this context. In everything else, we were standing shoulder-to-shoulder. We closed the deal to our mutual satisfaction. At the end, regardless our business relation, I used all my charms and tried to establish a different kind of relation with her, but this young lady recognized the problem on time, which ranked her in a category of serious players in both business and life; she politely thanked me for my time and left. I sighed deeply and got lost in my thoughts. We were aware of our mutual proficiency, I didn't show my enthusiasm (about her knowledge and her looks) during the meeting, I was really standing on my feet (even if it wasn't easy in some moments).

Still, this young lady, with her way of doing business, was sending only one message, not only to me, but also to everyone that she had meetings with, "Watch out guys, the women era is coming, we'll eat you up alive".

My opinion on this: "Finally, long-awaited and simply-perfect."

Can you take any good advices from this story?

I'll try to help you. Here are some advices:

REGECT THE STEREOTYPES, ACCEPT THE EQUALITY.

(This goes for all your beliefs that can be interpreted as stereotypes. Open your eyes, my dear Friends: is there really something that can

amaze you in these crazy times? For me there is not, like I said before, everything is possible and everything is impossible. No matter how deeply convinced you are in something, stop for a moment and think it through, maybe you are not right, and if you are, then think it through again, because even if you are right, sometimes it's necessary to take the plunge, after all you need to swim, otherwise befalls the drowning. For when it comes to equality to women, there's no need for more discussions or comments, the drama is over, naturally in favor of the fair sex. The acceptance of the equality can only make this life more exciting, believe me, I'm sick of the men being dangerous opponents, this way we still have an equally dangerous opponent but much easier on the eyes, simply perfect. Long live the equality!)

BUSINESS AND PLEASURE DON'T COME TOGHETHER

(Believe me, my dear Gentlemen, I know all about it. I'm sure that certainly, at least once, you had been tempted to mix business and pleasure. That's not a problem, feel free to do it, but first step out the business relation and the problem will be solved. I've explained to every employee in my company, that intimate relations inside the company are impossible, there are not forbidden, but unrealizable. Since that confused them, I tried to explain. I said that I could not forbid the intimate relationships to anyone, but what I can do is to fire those who have them, since an intimate relationship inside the organization means that the drops become the Niagara Falls. I know, since I have experience in that field as well. So Gentlemen, if there is chemistry with a certain colleague at work, so strong that the volcanoes will explode on both sides, and the boss of the company has no problem with it, then I'm asking you again to follow the same advice that I gave you in the begging. Never ever start an intimate relationship with a co-worker, believe me, already the next morning you'll see each other with different eyes, and you'll believe that you have more rights on each other than the day before, naturally, all that pulls a sea of drops, that have a chain reaction on accomplishing your duties efficiently. I know all about how love has no boundaries, how love doesn't choose the time, the love at the first sight, and blah, blah, blah; all I'm saying is to try to separate business from pleasure and you'll solve a serious problem. Trust the sinner on his word . . .)

LEARN FROM THE WOMEN

(At some point, during the carrier, every one of us experiences a lack of efficiency. Why is that? There are millions of reasons, and one of the most common is the tiredness of the work and the belief of being the best. I've already mentioned that you are far from being the best, there's always someone better than you, but there are times that we get distracted, and we don't even notice small details, usually very obvious and important for the work. In business, everything is important and you must take care of small details. Well, it's exactly there that women are fabulous. Women are much more thorough than we are; they are more devoted, and believe me, when they see a prey they bite much harder. After all, the lioness is hunting while the lion is sleeping; so trust me, she arouses much more fear than the big one who's only eating and sleeping, and who thinks than he's the king of the jungle. Efficient businesswomen understand work as putting on the make-up or wearing the mandatory high heels. It is natural and it has to be done correctly. Why do they care so much about the appearance? The efficient women attempt to be fantastic in everything, and naturally, everything starts from the appearance. I'll describe one of the common stereotypes in my dear Serbia, and it involves a man taking care of himself. A man who takes care of himself is usually described as metro sexual; they say he never leaves the gym and the beauty salons as if he was a woman, and that probably, he's gay. Can you imagine? I had a chance to experience it on my own skin, but why am I mentioning this? Dear Gentlemen, dear Comrades, leave the stereotypes and learn more from the women. Always think about how much attention they devote to themselves before they leave the house and go to work. I'm not saying that you need to act like a woman, for the start, double up the time that you want to devote to yourself and you'll see some fabulous resultants. Nobody is immune to beauty.

WOMEN ARE AWARE OF THEIR ABILITIES.

(All women are aware of the advantage they have over men; this advantage is their looks. Take it easy, this is not a stereotype. There's no man, not even one man, who can be indifferent to a beautiful woman. Most certainly, he'll be appreciating her taking care of herself, or he'll be admiring her beauty. It is like that, every man who's trying to deny it, is obviously lying.

Therefore, my dear Comrades, women are aware of their advantages and qualities, yet sometimes, they are not aware of their flaws, but that's one of the next stories. You must be careful, women are aware of how much they can achieve with their looks, charm, charisma and knowledge, so be sure that such a complete female person can always accomplish much more than a man. It's important that you have your goals in front of you, and that you respect the business methods and achievements of the person you are talking to, the charm and the good looks always complete the whole picture of the person, my compliments to that.

THE WOMEN'S ERA IS COMING.

(Many believe that it is already here, but that's not so true. I think that for me, it was very important to realize that women are equal, and in some cases, even more dangerous opponents than men. It is crucial to be aware of the fact that the women's era is coming and that is necessary to lower the guard and to let go to the flow. I know that many people don't share my opinion on equality, especially in the countries where the religion and the law are putting the women in the background, but that's a different story. Each one of my stories is meant to help you out in the business, although it doesn't give the precise guidelines about how you should deal with certain things; those precise guidelines you can learn them in college or by studying more the business publications. This is life, as I usually say, an already established issue, an already made mistake. That's why you should forget about the research, the religions, the laws and the customs; open your eyes and look around you, who knows, maybe tomorrow you'll end up in the role of the housewife, you never know, but get ready for anything, because the women are around the corner, all better, more intelligent and more dangerous. Anyway, it would be much easier if you accept it now than later when a woman takeovers your working place. Stand shoulder-to-shoulder and fight fairly, let the better one win, believe me, that's the only way.)

Just to remind you on the advices from this story:

- **REGECT THE STEREOTYPES, ACCEPT THE EQUALITY.**

- **BUSINESS AND PLEASURE DON'T COME TOGHETHER**

- **LEARN FROM THE WOMEN**

- **WOMEN ARE AWARE OF THEIR ABILITIES.**

- **THE WOMEN'S ERA IS COMING.**

7

PRIDE IS A DANGEROUS ENEMY

I will never forget certain images from my childhood and my teenage years. The environment that you are growing up is very important. In addition, it is very important to respect your parents for the things they were doing for you, and for all the trouble, they had to live through to accomplish it, and not to measure up your love by how much money they are ready to give you in certain moments. The way that you respect the others is coming from your house, in the similar way you respect your co-workers, your friends, your family, your wife and your children. Slowly but surely, you are growing to become a person who first of all respects himself and his family, admires the real values, and all this represents a healthy bases for further work. I always had, maybe even too much of respect for some people who didn't have any respect for me. Why do I mention again the family, the respectfulness, the rules of decent behavior, etc? The reasons are very simple: the conditions of my environment made me a businessman that I am today, but what shaped me the most are the persons who didn't have respect for themselves (at the same time, neither for me) and who spent their days like they were going to live million years. Not even the biggest and the most modern laptop could store all the humiliation, the mocking, the dispraise, and the distrust that I've suffered; naturally, not from everyone, but

from certain individuals, who I have to thank the most. Thank you for showing me how I should not be (this also has to be known, noticed and learned) and for making me stronger than ever, by your behavior. Believe me, even now that I'm writing this, I still hear, running through my mind, thousands of ugly remarks, humiliations and mistrusts on my account, but I've always accepted all this as a challenge or competition, that's what held me back, helped me not to give up. This was a very long introduction, for a short life story, which brings along important messages.

I've already told you that I was working in concrete blocks manufacture. It was a bloody and heavy work; all day long I was making war with the most primitive machine for producing the blocks that you ever seen. Thank God, it was using the electricity and not the oxen. It was a summer day, the temperature was over 35°C, and I was already approaching the daily planned quote, so I was washing out the tools. One of the suppliers was late all day with a white cement delivery, of course, when I was about to leave, he miraculously showed up. I didn't complain much (even if I did, it wouldn't make much difference), but I started suffocating from the fatigue and the drops. I wasn't really planning to carry the cement at the end of the workday, naturally manually and alone, since the help worker left, but I had no choice. There were more than twenty sacks of white cement on the parking lot in front of my manufacture. While I was carrying it, sack by sack, the neighbors were passing by on their way from work; they were looking at me with contempt, some of them didn't even say hello, and the majority was in complete shock, "Why is he doing all this, when by Serbian standards, he's a rich man?", they were wondering. I didn't mind those looks; an empty wallet was much a bigger problem for me. Upon this, a car stopped, but I couldn't immediately see who was inside, since I was suffocating from the dust. It was a friend of mine, I use to spend a lot of time with him, but he could never understand why is it that I decided to do a job like this. (You should consider my young age, I've barely got out the teenage days, many would be humiliated by the job that I was doing, but not me) He was well dressed; without even saying a proper hello, he immediately said, "My god, you're such an idiot, wasting all your time with those blocks." In that moment, a sack of white cement got ripped, so imagine what I looked like, it was very embarrassing, but I smiled gently, and told him that we will speak later, since I was busy. I finished everything quickly and went home.

My dear Friends, I am far from being a giant, but I'm on the right path in achieving my goals much before the deadlines. I was never embarrassed about a job, I was always doing several jobs at one time, I always stubbornly persisted to accomplish my goals, to many I became a role model, both in business and in education (don't worry, not when it comes to marriages). I overtook many big players, while the proud ones, who were making fun of me, don't even have the guts to say hello now. I really like it when I see an opponent so proud, who thinks it's beneath his dignity to do some jobs, because that means that he's vulnerable, and vulnerable preys are the easiest to capture. Pride's most faithful companions, like the shame, the embarrassment, the superiority and inferiority complexes, etc, can become your worst enemies. Don't let you pride make you become an easy prey. When pride rules over you, it is very easy to notice and many people will try to use it against you (I would be the first to notice it and I would know where to hit you). However, when you show that nothing scares you and that there's no job that can embarrass you when you have a goal to accomplish, in that case you are considered being a dangerous rival, since they know that you're clever enough to rule over your pride, and not let the pride rule over you.

Can you take any good advices from this story?

I'll try to help you. Here are some advices:

THERE'S NO SHAME IN ANY JOB.

(Maybe some of you wouldn't agree, but there's no shame in any job, whether you like it or not, whether you want it or not. In the begging of the carrier, many of us did jobs that we didn't like (some still do), trying to convince themselves they would do this job for a short period, and that they would change it for a job they really like and that suits them well. Some people spend the whole life doing jobs they don't like. Do you really think I liked waking up 6 o'clock in the morning and working until 5 PM in the manufacture of concrete blocks? Of course, I didn't, but I thought I could use it as a springboard for what I really wanted to do. I was simultaneously doing two different jobs, and sometimes-even three. Whenever I stepped on the concrete block production line or I entered the gym to help people exercise, I always took a deep breath, prayed to god to pass the day without any injuries, thought of higher goals and repeated constantly: "There's no shame in any job."

WHAT DOESN'T KILL YOU, MAKES YOU STRONGER

(I know that you already heard this before and that this sentence is fairly known. My dear Friends, it really is that way. After each meeting that I held, after each job that I did, I learned many things and became much more experienced than before, and what this experience determined were those very things that didn't kill me, but made me stronger. The thing that made you stronger is the power of the gained experience; I believe you would pay a fortune to have it before entering some business or in the beginning of your carrier. Those situations that didn't "kill" me became very precious now, in other words, when I find myself in the similar or same situation, I always know the final result—I'll be winner of the new battle.)

EFFORT ALWAYS PAYS OUT.

(It can be a very powerful weapon, regardless your work field, if you carefully direct the energy towards the specific target. It is particularly important for the business people, because only with big efforts and commitment you can achieve the set goals. I would also like to mention, that not only you are going to achieve your goals, but also you will have a chance to become expert in certain field, which could help you out a lot in the further development of your career. I know this might sound like reading from a management textbook, but think about it for a while, there's no such thing as useless effort, only the useful one, in one way or the other.)

VEERING OFF THE ROAD DISTANCES YOU MORE FROM YOUR GOAL.

(This might be a bit strong word, or should I say, advice for the above-mentioned example, but I personally experienced that one drop can provoke the flood. Therefore, if you do something, do it right, and try to be as good as you can, because the moment that you wonder off, or you pass to another job, this is exactly where you start moving away from the accomplishment of the previously started job. It doesn't matter if you make the concrete blocks or a business plan for a specific project, set your priorities, stray from your everyday responsibilities only if it would help you accomplish faster the set goals.)

MILAN DIMITRIJEVIC

BE PROUD ONLY OF THE FACT THAT YOU ARE NOT A PROUD PERSON.

(It is not enough to agree and approve this statement; you need also to apply it. Pride is a dangerous enemy and it can affect in the large matter the accomplishment of everyday responsibilities, both private and work related. I trust that you are a top manager, a General Manager, a PHD, an honest man, etc, but my dear Friends, don't put it in the forefront, and don't tire the people around with your title and your profession. The top personalities and those that accomplish well their private and work obligations, they don't need special introduction, fast enough, they become well known, and people pay much more attention to these people than to braggers, narcissists, or in better words—to the proud ones.)

Just to remind you on the advices from this story:

- **THERE'S NO SHAME IN ANY JOB.**

- **WHAT DOESN'T KILL YOU, MAKES YOU STRONGER**

- **EFFORT ALWAYS PAYS OUT.**

- **VEERING OFF THE ROAD DISTANCES YOU MORE FROM YOUR GOAL.**

- **BE PROUD ONLY OF THE FACT THAT YOU ARE NOT A PROUD PERSON.**

8

WRONG BUS

I made the majority of the mistakes in my life when I wasn't listening to myself. Every time I have a dilemma, or if I find myself face-to-face with a problem, I try to get the biggest benefit with the least damage (now you probably think, well done, you discovered the hot water!). When you have a problem, there's always a damage involved, and it's only a question of how much trace it would leave on you and on your future ventures. After a battle, everyone is a general and everyone is a wiseacre, but there are times when we find ourselves in apparently hopeless situation, which demands a wise decision and not the wrong bus. What does a bus have to do now with a whole story? A wise man said, "If you enter the wrong bus, every stop is the wrong one." There's so much wisdom in this simple sentence. It's so perfect. My dear Friends, if you were following this sentence, you will avoid many drop dashes that could occur, not only because of the wrong bus, but also because of the wrong stop where you are waiting for the bus.

In business (and in life), it is very important how you choose the projects that naturally, have to bring you profit, that will naturally, lead you a step further to the goal, that you've naturally, set long ago. It is all very natural, but there are times we become so preoccupied and obsessed by the goals achievement, that we don't even realize that we are at the wrong

bus stop, waiting for the bus that apparently goes to the desired direction, but don't forget, all the next stops are wrong. Sometimes, the wrong bus seems so good, that it would make you think that you are at least the management guru, you'd be proud of the good deal that you've made, but this is only a delusion, which will put you to despair and will make you do even more desperate moves. In life, there are different people that we encounter, different opportunities, and there are many jobs that we can accomplish with these people. One thing is the accomplishment of the job, but the consequences are another. Occasionally, it is very easy to enter a job and very difficult to leave it without consequences. Naturally, I already mentioned that there are always consequences (always try to have as few as possible), but there are times they can be disastrous. A certain situation left a deep trace in my life; its consequences affected in large matter my private life as well.

One of my friends called Zorko was late for the afternoon coffee meeting with me. He explained that he was on a business meeting with a person of our age. Zorko said that he seemed to be a lot like us, involved in business, well educated, owner of a good company, and above all this, "Likes to go out, likes to have fun, likes beautiful girls, in other words, he likes the same things that you like, you are very similar", said Zorko. "Zorko, you know that I'm difficult when it comes to new night life buddies, it takes time, however to get to know a person and then to go out together, I'd like to know at least something about him", I explained to Zorko. Since it was Saturday, and Saturdays are always reserved for "artistic creativities" (another expression that I like to use for the nightlife), Zorko knew it, since he was my faithful companion. The afternoon coffee was a ritual that we had so we could organize where and with whom to go out with. Zorko then asked, in low voice, if it would be a problem to bring along to the club his new buddy tonight, even if I didn't know him, he tried to reassure me about that guy, he said that he was an educated person and a good business contact. I don't know why, but I said, "Why not".

That night I met Klada, at the first sight he seemed an educated young man with a lot of positive energy. I don't want to get into the details about the way I like to have fun at the clubs, but I'm quite a showman, and I really like to dance and get rid of the negative energy. I thought that Klada would be shy and hesitating, but on the contrary, we spent that night like we were friends forever. As the time was passing, we were going out more frequently, and our friendship grew stronger. One evening, Klada and I were sitting at the table, and he overheard the conversation that I had on

the telephone; it was about me asking the other person to delay the signing of the contract for a week, because it was then that the money was supposed to come, since I haven't collected enough money as we had agreed. After the conversation, Klada offered to borrow me the money that I needed, by explaining that he knows how much it would mean to me, and even if we don't know each other for a long time, he had enough confidence in me that I would return the money. Under the circumstances, I made a decision and I agreed to borrow the money from Klada. That was the place, my Dears, where I embarked the wrong bus. In less than a week, I returned the borrowed money to Klada, but he knew me well enough to know how much I'll appreciate that gesture, and how that situation would strengthen considerably the friendship that just started.

As time was passing, we spent more and more time together, and we knew more and more things about each other. We were giving advices to one another, we were using each other's contacts, and we were making plans, spending time and strengthening the relationship that was slowly becoming a true friendship. It's a rather long story, countless situations from our friendship could be useful for you, but I'll try to make it as short as possible.

During our ritual Sunday lunch, excited by the story about the Saturday night and probably enthusiastic about the fact that we actually had a very good life, Klada said that we should start a common project. My projects were mainly the construction of the business-residential premises and Klada wanted us to construct one of those together (not so much for the profit, as for the reinforcement of our friendship and our positions). I was taken by the emotions and the friendship and so I said, "Why not?" (Although long time ago I had said, that whatever I'd do in life I'd do it alone, without having a partner). I never doubted a second our business project would be accomplished successfully, and we'd make a good profit, but the problem was not in business, since we were going really well, but in our way of living. Klada is a young man, full of verve but with too many inferiority complexes, which he was trying to overcome in worst possible way—with alcohol. We all liked to have a drink sometimes, but we also tried to behave ourselves when we were drinking. His behavior slowly started to ruin my good image. During our friendship I was known (in public) as a fair guy who knows very well how to behave himself, and even if I was going out a lot, my job and the achievement of the set goals were never questioned. The problems were becoming bigger and bigger, while the business and the friendship, when not under the influence of alcohol, were becoming better

and better. At one point, I wanted to stop everything but I just couldn't, the project accomplishment, but also all the responsibilities towards different target groups were mutual, and on the other side, our friendship was so strong that I considered him family.

One day, under different circumstances (particularly bad), Klada initiated a big problem, and we both could lose our lives, but fortunately, it ended with no tragic consequences. That moment triggered the begging of the end. Three years of friendship were destroyed as fast as it took us to know each other. When time came to settle our accounts (although in time we've launched not one, but three common projects, that each was supposed to be accomplished from the profit of the previous one, even though not even the first project was yet completed), Klada showed his real face. The results of the meeting with his lawyers were the following: I took upon myself all the obligations (even if I didn't have to, and there were no legal bases) as well as the project completion. As far as the other projects, Klada demanded the immediate refund of the invested money, as he didn't want to work with me anymore, etc, etc, etc. Consequently, dear Gentlemen, my office was a Niagara Flood, I couldn't believe what I just experienced, and it was entirely my fault. I accepted all the terms, even if the termination of the business cooperation coasted me almost million dollars, I gained much more on the other side. It was upon me to complete three more projects; in short period of time I had to find a big amount of money that was supposed to bring me even bigger amount (but that was the risk) so I could manage to pull it trough. My dear Friends, it was not easy, I just couldn't stop the bus that was still going in the wrong direction, but after a long struggle, I managed to get out at an unfamiliar bus stop and try to fix the things.

My friendship with Klada was the most expensive experience of my life, but after all that, I can only be thankful, since I know that if I could turn back time, I wouldn't have a chance to buy for million dollars the gained experience that would also save me even more money. By the way, believe it or not, short after the end of our cooperation, Klada lost his own, millions worth company, and changed his life big time (in the business terms). What stayed the same, what he could never change, was his attraction to alcohol, in other words, his wrong bus that he had embarked long time a go and could not get out anymore.

Can you take any good advices from this story?

I'll try to help you. Here are some advices:

CAREFULLY CHOOSE THE STOP WHERE YOU'LL WAIT FOR THE BUS.

(Many times we enter the business without planning the details or analyzing different circumstances, and even more important, without considering the worst-case scenario, but really the worst one. If you enter every job by considering the worst-case scenario, by anticipating the worst thing that could happen to you in this job, believe me, you won't be having trouble dealing with any kind of problem. That's why it is very important to know on whose door you want to knock and whose number to dial. At that moment, you must think that everybody is against you, and that everything will go wrong (I know it sounds a bit paranoid, but we'll discuss paranoia later), so you must examine in detail every side of the problem. My dear Friends, there's one thing that you particularly need to take care of—every bus stop that you approach, seems attractive and there's an information on each one of them that says it's exactly there that stops the bus that you need. However, I'm telling this from my personal experience, sometimes you need to pass by even hundred stops to get to the right one, but when you get to the right stop, not only you will sit on the right bus, but also every following stop will be the right one as well.)

IT IS DIFFICULT TO GET OUT THE WRONG BUS.

(No truth is greater than this one; sometimes people never get out of the wrong bus and experience the worst-case scenario. If you didn't read very carefully the above story, read it again, and then once again. This might be one of the most important lessons that I wrote to you, in particular since the wrong bus pulls out a number of other things that are wrong as well. It is quite important to mention that nothing is easy in that bus that seems so beautiful and "profitable", actually it's very difficult to achieve the set goals, and try to imagine how you will feel when you realize that you are in the wrong bus, and that you need to get off urgently. Well, now, there are two very important things. First: when you realize where you are and what you are doing, and you fervently wish to get off, then you start grabbing towards the exit and put everything else aside, which is in the human nature, but that's not the way it goes. It is very difficult to put aside million of already started responsibilities, and just run away. What does it

say about you then? Are you someone who runs away from the difficulty? No, no, no, my Dears, it doesn't work this way, and it is not possible in real life. You're going to have to finish everything that you've started and only then, you can ask the driver to stop the bus so you can get off, because there's a huge whirl that constantly tries to push you back inside. Second: the line between good and bad is like the line between love and hate; it is very thin, almost invisible. Why am I mentioning this? It is very important that during the conflict you save your mental health, as well as your close ones and yourself. If you lose your mind, you could easily cross the line of the right and honest, and I would never recommend that. You have to gather the last particles of your strength, to send depression on a long holiday; if you don't see the light at the end of the tunnel, than make one and walk with slow and careful steps towards that light, or in other words towards the exit of the bus. Dear Friends, seriously consider what I've just told you, it's not a joke; the consequences of the wrong bus can be vast. Another thing, I almost forgot: I don't know what you are going to do when you leave the bus, you might be broke and the situation could be desperate, but there's one good thing in this whole story, at least you will know how to recognize the right bus station. The station where the right buses stop, the buses that go to the directions that you want, that halt on the stops that you want and you never have problem to get off. I know, it sounds almost unbelievable, but I'm saying this from my own experience, it's a magnificent feeling to get off the wrong bus, and even better, when you recognize the next one for being wrong, so you elegantly pass it by.

FRIENDSHIP AND BUSINESS DON'T GO TOGETHER

(I don't know if anyone will agree with this advice, but I repeat, this is my opinion, and it's a product (as it turned out) of long research and earned experience. For that reason, even if you don't want to follow it, or if your best friend is your business partner, try to think for at least a moment at the worst-case scenario, and then try to decide which is more valuable to you, your friend or your job, the job that your family depends on. It is very difficult, especially if it's a good friend and you have a harmonious relation; but trust me, there are many solutions how you can work together and don't get too much hurt, if someone stops following the right path. I don't know about you, but I personally like to spend time with my friends, and I'm always there to help; as for the clients, I do business with them, and I

wouldn't like to mix again those two things. That is one of worse versions of the wrong bus that is extremely difficult to exit, yet we usually enter it in a jiffy.)

THE SMART ONES ARE FEARFUL

(I've been told many times that I worry too much about some things, that I'm paranoid and that I'm anxious for no reason. Every time, but really, every single time, when somebody says that I'm fearful, I respond, "The smart ones are fearful". There are different situations in life that bring us to make different moves, whose results we are only about to see. I am afraid of doing something wrong, of damaging somebody or accidently causing someone pain in neglect. Where is this coming from, what does it have to do with business? Everything that you do, I repeat, affects your family and the people around you. Not everybody thinks the same way, and most of the people go around without thinking twice and giving much importance to the magnificent question: *what if? What if*, is the question asked by smart people, who think about more things in business, than just completing the project and making profit. Both positive and negative fears (positive for the good things—whether we'll make more or less money, and negative for the bad things—whether the business can put someone in danger) have to be present in analyzing every business. Everyone is afraid of something, there's fear in everyone, yet it happens sometimes that this fears disappear when most needed to be present and it's exactly then that we make a mistake. It's not a question of cowardice here, don't get me wrong, it's about doing business thoroughly, one thing that we try to accomplish in these crazy times, and all in purpose of not becoming crazy ourselves. In business, it is healthy to be fearful, it's even essential. That kind of thinking will only strengthen your way of making the decision, which is not so bad.)

ALWAYS BE READY FOR THE WORST
AND EXPECT THE BEST.

(I've already brought up this topic in the previous advices. To be ready for the worst refers to the projection of the worst-case scenario, or in other words the situation when you project the worst possible thing that could happen from the deal that you made, and in the second place if you find yourself in

that situation, how you're going to get out of it. This isn't something new, I know that, yet many people around us occasionally get too optimistic about a business deal, and simply don't believe that something could go wrong. My dear Friends, there's always something that could go wrong, although you would handle it much easier if you had predicted it, and if you hadn't, then you slowly start to drown in drops flood. We all expect the best, both from business and life, but put that aside and create the strategy according to the worst-case scenario. In that way you will be much more familiar to the fact that the results could be unfavorable, yet sometimes they can be magnificent. Once more, it's all up to you.)

SPEAK NO ILL OF THE DEAD

(This is a very important rule, always speak well of others and especially of the dead. "Why now the dead, who is dead?" many would ask. Obviously, I am not talking about the dead people, but about the living ones that we burry in our heads. I know, I know, it does sound cruel, although, some might even find it harmless, but let me explain. Each one of us has a person that hurt him, deceived him, did wrong or similar. In most cases, we have common friends, and usually when we get together with them, the conversation starts about the person that you don't have a nice opinion of, so you act emotionally and pronounce the worst possible words about that person. My first question: is it necessary to say all this in that way? Of course, it's not. You have to be like Switzerland, neutral, saying that you don't mean bad to anyone and that simply you don't have any comments. If it happens that someone still insists that you state your opinion, say that you run your business in a certain way, the person in question in another, so you could never agree and naturally, you wish him all the best. This is the way to talk and this kind of attitude speaks a lot about you, as a person and as a businessman. You show being a diplomatic person and not a gossiper; you go forward, you stand still on your feet, your results speak for themselves, you don't return to past but you head to the future. This is important: simply erase this person as if he never existed, burry him in your head; however find the strength and wish him all the best, in public and inside you. It is a liberating experience and a magnificent feeling.)

Just to remind you on the advices from this story:

- **CAREFULLY CHOOSE THE STOP WHERE YOU'LL WAIT FOR THE BUS.**

- **IT IS DIFFICULT TO GET OUT THE WRONG BUS.**

- **FRIENDSHIP AND BUSINESS DON'T GO TOGETHER**

- **THE SMART ONES ARE FEARFUL**

- **ALWAYS BE READY FOR THE WORST AND EXPECT THE BEST.**

- **SPEAK NO ILL OF THE DEAD**

9

ARE YOU READY TO BE AN EQUERRY?

My dear Friends, it is beyond all question that I love my city (Belgrade) and my country (Serbia), it is natural since it's the place where I come from and where my family is. All through my short life, from all the jobs (or ideas, if you like) that I had started, two jobs suppressed all the others and kept all my attention. Not purposely, yet the first job is directed to business development and the second to personal development. You are probably asking the question: isn't the business development also a personal one?

A short answer to that question: IT IS NOT.

A different story explains this argument, but I've mentioned it because my personal development is related to frequent travelling. Fortunately for me, I had a chance to visit many countries and cities (from US to Australia) and every city had different attractions and was magnificent in its own way. I don't know why, but I always avoided London. From primitive stories told by even more primitive people, I heard that it was always raining in London, that it's nothing special and similar, and I was, as it seems, even more primitive than them, since I believed people who

were spreading different stories, while never in their life they'd left their countries. Again, it was my mistake, but it doesn't matter. After taking my Master degree, without much thought, I decided to pursue a PhD degree. Consulting with a friend (a professor who did his PhD at the University of Cambridge), I realized that the begging of my research work (as well as the end) should be in the rainy, and not so interesting city of London. In spite of the circumstances and the bad stories, I decided to go to London as soon as possible and start the research. Unbelievably, London had a huge influence on me, therefore on my decisions as well, which dragged series of other decisions, which naturally, changed my life forever.

Gentlemen, it is very simple, when someone mentions London, the first thing on my mind is POWER. A magnificent union of history and tradition, while every corner reminds you of the wealth of this nation, and the position held by the Great Britain among the most powerful countries of the world. In each angle of that city, I had an exceptional feeling, which thought me much more that I was ready to acknowledge in that moment. Does all this sound a bit confusing and philosophic? I apologize, but soon you will realize what are the reasons London changed my life. Everything I saw in London, everything I did, all the things I experienced or lived through, everything held only one massage, or better said one word: POWER. You are probably wondering, "Why power?" Power is something very easy to recognize at others; when you realize that you are much weaker than your opponent is, you change your behavior, and you either withdraw, since you know that you will lose, or you stubbornly persist and try to stand shoulder-to-shoulder with the mighty opponent. For an unknown reason, London became my opponent. I was overjoyed. I always used to say, "If there is something that you don't know you have to ask", and now I say, "If you want to see something powerful and at the same time, you want to see how powerful you are, simply go to London." No matter where you are coming from and how rich you are, in London you are always a beginner. How come?

One sunny day, a billionaire and his entourage knocked on the door of the prestige private member club in London. The polite staff opened the door and asked the Gentleman what he wanted, since they didn't know him. The Gentleman expressed the wish to speak with a person on a higher status than was the battler, so he could get the information about the membership. Confused, the battler asked, "You need information about the membership?" The Gentleman responded proudly, "Yes, of course, and hurry up, I don't have time to argue all day here with you."

The battler politely asked the Gentleman to wait, so he could call someone from higher status. After 15 minutes of waiting, the battler came back and politely announced that for the moment, no one has time to receive the Gentleman, and that this wasn't the right admitting procedure. Clearly irritated, the Gentleman asked the battler, "Don't you know who are you talking to? I could buy everything that you have here!" The battler answered politely, "Dear Sir, for you to become a member of this club you need to be recommended by someone, and even if you get recommended, the club Council has to decide by majority rule whether you'll be received or not. Under my estimation, even if they accept you, which I doubt, and even if you find someone to recommend you, your position in the club definitely won't be the one that you enjoy in the society at the present. My great-grandfather was a worker in horse stables, my grandfather was a gardener, my father an equerry, and I am a battler now. By the way, believe it or not, I'm a millionaire, but in this club there are things bigger than money: the tradition, the history, the trust, the knowledge, the vision, the common goal and of course, the power that we acquired over the centuries, and not in 5 minutes, like you wished to by getting the membership. You know where the way out is. Goodbye!"

Ouch, that was uncomfortable! I don't know why, but this story made me feel powerless. I wonder how the proud billionaire felt after that incident. My dear Friends, I accidently overheard this story over a diner in London. I'm not saying that I was snooping on the next table, it was simple impossible not to hear. The man who told the story is the best friend of the battler from the story, and the reason he told the whole story was that his friends were annoying him by wanting to become members of that club. Naturally, with this story, he nicely explained the situation, while I remained completely shocked.

My dear Friends, you have to be careful when you knock on someone's door. The feeling that the billionaire had at the door of that club that day, was the same feeling that I had trough my whole sojourn in London. I wish all the best for my family, which is natural, but for a moment, I was devastated by all the things that I saw. Quickly, I came to my senses and made some very important decisions in my life. I was born a fighter, and I'll die like one. All the obstacles are opportunities for me. London is one of my challenges and opportunities. In my country, I know where I stand, but in London, I don't know if I could apply for a position of the stable worker or the equerry. The billionaire never came back to that club, probably he furiously bought several buildings in London and opened his own private

club; nevertheless, I constantly keep coming back to London. Do you know why? Unintentionally, I knocked on the door of the new world, where the entering ticket for the high society is very expensive; in my own way I'll try to find my place in the sun, and I don't have other options than to succeed. If what it takes is to be an equerry, then why not, I made concrete blocks and that brought me to incredible sites, where would I then get by working as an equerry, especially in London?

I have only one question for you: are you ready to be an equerry?

Can you take any good advices from this story?

I'll try to help you. Here are some advices:

TRY TO BE THE FIRE, BOTH BIG AND SMALL.

(My dear Friends, I know well that not everybody is capable of becoming successful and rich, but everybody is capable of trying their best to reach out the heights. Apparently, it is in the nature of the big "players", as I like to call them, always to want more and never to be satisfied with what they have. This is natural, because sky is the limit, but what about us, who are constantly trying to become big? However, it's very time-consuming, therefore slowly but surely, the years go by and we are losing hope. Actually, it is very simple, try to be the fire, follow the fire path, since it is the only way to become noticed, regardless if you are a big or a small fire, in either way, you can burn, and this is what is valued in the business world. Maybe all this might sound a bit confusing, but I'll simplify. Me, for example, I don't believe that I would reach Trump or Gates, those are still unimaginable heights for me, probably it goes the same for many of you, however dear Friends, both you and I, as well as Trump and Gates, we are all on the same path, it's just that some have advanced more than others. You need to follow the fire path and never turn off that path, and then it would only be a question of time when you will start surpassing, when others will start appreciating or fearing your heat.)

THERE ARE ALWAYS MORE POWERFUL PEOPLE.

(This is a much known thing and everybody is aware of it, however some people tend to forget it. First comes crawling, then comes walking, then running, and if you are very good, you will probably fly. Please,

try not to fall too fast, since that is the common scenario for those who think they're the most powerful ones. Intentionally I'm using the term most powerful because it's exactly how people feel in certain moments, when money makes them irrational and they start to believe they could do anything. Naturally, I repeat, I'm writing all this from my personal experience. Do try to be powerful, that's all right, just don't pretend to be the most powerful, it could put you in big problems; the least that could happen is that you be humiliated like a billionaire from my story. In any case, always keep in mind that there are people who are more powerful than you, and don't try testing your power in the wrong way, instead try placing it in the right direction. It will only make you more powerful, nothing else.)

RESPECT OTHERS SO THEY WOULD RESPECT YOU.

(I've learned this long ago and I never discriminated people, regardless their position in the company, society or family. Many people think they are more important than the others; it's all right, but first you have to be really important, and second, don't rub it on anyone's nose. You will manage it, if you start by doing simple things, like politely saying hello to your concierge or to the doorman in your company, by having lunch with your driver or coffee with the maid. Those moments consume very little of your time, yet you couldn't believe the kind of effect they make. I know, I know, you are all probably thinking that what I'm saying is a natural thing, but exactly this natural thing is what many people don't do, yet they expect respect and politeness from the people they don't show neither respect nor politeness. Me, on the other hand, I have a problem with that. Unfortunately, in my country, when you are polite and you kindly greet everyone, people look funny at you, as if you were at least insane. Do you know why it's like that? They're simply not used to people being kind and polite. That's not the case only in my country, but from all the countries that I've visited and where I worked, I felt it in my country stronger than else. For a moment, I will compare some things and sum up this advice. It's very easy to look down from the height, same as being a fool and choosing the easy way, though it's very difficult to come down to earth and consider all the people the same way, because it is equally difficult as being smart and choosing the hard way. Where do you think you would have better results? When you answer yourself that question, answer also to the following one:

"How would all this influent my business results?" You already know my answer, so don't just be aware of yours, but apply it as well.)

WEIGHT CAREFULLY THE DECISIONS REGARDING THE FUTURE.

(Beloved Friends, this naturally does not apply to small decisions, like buying a car or a refrigerator (although some people might have to weight also for that), but for bigger decisions that involve your future and the future of your family. People hardly support changes and they're typically scared by the question "WHAT IF?" That's how it should be; yet, does everything have to end with this question? Are you going to spend the rest of your life in pronouncing the same question and doing nothing? Some probably are, but I'm not, and neither are all those who follow my advices; we firmly say NO to that. This is a very important advice; take time to think about your plans for the future, make sure those plans involve also your family future, namely your children's future. Am I asking too much? Does it sound too far? My dear Gentlemen, everything that you do can affect the future of your children; this is why it is important that as parent, you'll be able to help your child one day, and not to downgrade him or her with your past activities. London is one of my destinations, I saw challenge and problem in it, just like when I first started the construction of my first building and was completely broke. I repeat again, if once you are a fighter, you'll always be a fighter, but leave this apart. The future was never closer; so, open your eyes and take a deep breath, then make a step, a carefully calculated step, that will lead you in the desired direction.)

RENUNCIATION GIVES BRILLIANT RESULTS.

(This advice is also strongly connected to your ability to manage the changes, in other words, to tolerate them. Imagine for a moment, that everything you are currently doing is running excellent and that everything you have is fantastic. However, opposite to the others, you come to realize that you must leave all that, and go on a trip where you will have to create everything from scratch, since it's the best decision for your future, and the future of your family. Many people would ask, probably your close ones as well, "why is it that you took such a decision, when you have

everything a man could desire, a nice house, a car, a job, a family . . . ?" I'll tell you what I think. When someone would say that to me, and it already happened several times, I listened very carefully, but I knew I was listening to people who don't stand the changes, and who are afraid of them. I'm saying all this because I travelled the world, and realized there are places where I should try to make my future; the kind of future, I definitely don't see in my country. You already know all that, maybe also some American guy would say he likes Brazil or Mexico or Italy, that he wants to try it out there, but why did he say that? It's very simple, he saw the opportunity and he's not afraid to use it. In the end, it all brings as back to that magnificent word—*renunciation,* or—*sacrifice,* if you prefer. Everything that I sacrificed in life, and everything that I renounced from, for the sake of higher goals, it always paid out. Dear Friends, not all the people are prepared to sacrifice themselves and change their way of living. It's very simple: if I didn't renounce all these things in my life, who knows where I would be now, probably where I started from, I believe it hundred percent; but since I decided to choose the hard way, I've reached unthinkable heights that I could only dream of when I first started doing business. Renunciation gives brilliant results; if you don't trust me, and you are too scared to try, then for the start, ask others or read about it, there are many of us who said NO to apparently impossible thinks; many people understood renunciation and sacrificing as a tool for achieving the higher goals, and nothing else.)

Just to remind you on the advices from this story:

- **TRY TO BE THE FIRE, BOTH BIG AND SMALL.**

- **THERE ARE ALWAYS MORE POWERFUL PEOPLE.**

- **RESPECT OTHERS SO THEY WOULD RESPECT YOU.**

- **WEIGHT CAREFULLY THE DECISIONS REGARDING THE FUTURE.**

- **RENUNCIATION GIVES BRILLIANT RESULTS.**

10

SETTING GOALS IS A SOUL REMEDY

My dear Friends, I'm trying to offer you some guidelines; no matter what position you have in the company, may you have your own company, or may you be unemployed. Through frequent life/business problems, that I have lived or am still living, I'll try to facilitate the accomplishment of your everyday responsibilities, may you be the general manager or the shopkeeper.

Most of you would like to know the secret of growing rich, or the way to make millions and don't become insane. Most of you would like to know the secret of successful business. Most of you would like to know the secret about how to become an influential and powerful person. Most of you would like earn billions by reading one book (like this one, or similar), ok maybe by reading several books, that each costs a couple of dollars. How nice is this, nice and foolish! Most of you are wondering now, "Why doesn't this kid stop prating and starts showing us the directives how to become top leaders or managers, and next to that how to earn a couple of millions?" Some of you logically think: "Well, if he can earn that much in that age, I can make double than." That's the way to go, me too I say the same thing, but let's just stop for a moment with all those millions.

My Dears, the secret of the success is not in the books. Books are the guidelines, the sources of the wisdom; they help you not to get off the right path. However, in your movie, you are the one who has the leading role, and all the wise or foolish decisions that you make will best present the movie genre i.e. if it is an action movie with a happy end, or a tragedy where simply everything is tragic. Thousands of read books will never make you a millionaire, however your decisions will have the support of the thousands books, the support that is essential for you to become a millionaire.

The secret of the success lies in every person on this planet, while me, as well as others like me, we are trying to help you find the right path. It is necessary to find yourself; you need to work on your self-knowledge, so you could explore your nature in the right way. (I firmly suggest that you read one of my favorite books on this topic, wrote by Mister Robin Sharma: "The Monk Who Sold His Ferrari", and if you had read it, then read it again, and after some time once again, trust me, it's a great recipe for motivation and self-knowledge). The key of your success lies in your nature. There's no test in this world that could determine the real essence of your nature, the thing that would make you the number 1; however it could help you discover your affinities, but the thing that you do the best, you must find it inside yourself. You wonder how to do it? Some realize it early, some late, some spend their whole lives in delusion that they do the job made exactly for them. Naturally, it is important that you do the job that you like, and that makes you happy, and if you can also live well from that job, then you've sold a big life problem. Many people had found themselves, and they are more than pleased with their lives, I don't know almost any, but I know they exist. However, much more frequent are those who still wonder, and still face the dilemmas, for both personal and job matters. We have many examples from the practices of the world's biggest leaders, entrepreneurs, scientists. They had studied the half of their lives for one profession, and then they've realized their real nature, and became something completely different. It's difficult not to adore the story of Bill Gates, or the one of the slightly older gentleman, Mr. Mark McCormack. I don't doubt that Bill Gates would be a great lawyer, doctor, or politician, yet as a leader, visionary, entrepreneur, and a man far beyond his time, he found himself early enough and became a number 1 in the IT industry. On the other hand, Mark McCormack, while working as attorney, he probably kept thinking about golf, and the way to realize his dreams. For the start, he left the advocacy and directed his energy to the accomplishment of the set goals, and he managed to reach unthinkable heights. Several times,

he mentioned that it was very hard, but he didn't want to quit, he had discovered himself and he knew he would succeed.

Personally, I can't say I completely explored myself (hang on, I'm still a young boy, I'm only 28) and I wouldn't say I precisely know that the job I do is the right thing for me. I do things I like and things I don't, yet on my short journey I perceived myself so deeply that I know that I will never run away from the problems, and will always give my best to achieve my goals. Yes, my Dears: goals, goals and only goals. Goals are a soul remedy and a terrific self-knowledge initiator. Stop reading for a moment and think about how many set goals do you have at present, both family and business related. To be honest, many people get confused when I mention this sentence. My goals are constantly growing, I divide them in short-term and long-term goals, but the most important thing, which many people find absurd, is the fact that I currently have 87 set goals (short-term, long-term, personal and business—all together). Some people around me often ask me what do I consider a goal and why I have so many goals.

My dear Friends, we are all very different, and we all have very different ways of thinking. Some may want to buy a new car, a watch, a new house or similar, some have the ambition to become the best chemists of the world, etc. The most important thing is to keep increasing your goal list, because the goals are unbelievable initiators and motivators. I feel incredible when I take my goal list and cross off the one that I just have accomplished. Since I started to work, I've accomplished some goals much before foreseen, but I quickly set new ones. If it happens that I despond, I just look up for my goal list, which always says that I don't have time to lose and there's so much work to do.

Can you take any good advices from this story?

I'll try to help you. Here are some advices:

GOOD HUSBANDRY PRACTICE IS CRUCIAL.

(This was the very essence of doing business in times of the Kingdome of Babylon, and it still is today. It is necessary that you practice good husbandry in both business and life. What does it actually mean to practice "good husbandry"? Using the good husbandry techniques principally means doing business based on healthy foundations. Any different behavior would lead you to problems. You must put your business on healthy foundations and choose healthy projects, and the most important thing is to use the

project results for creating new projects. Why do I say that? You cannot spend the money you don't have and call yourself a wise person and top businessperson. I am very aware of the fact that most of the big business projects are based on the loans of state funds, investors or banks. No matter how stable the market, you can never know what tomorrow brings, but regardless the uncertainty you need to pay back the bank. Don't get me wrong, getting a loan is a natural thing, but only for period of time, same like you being the beginner in business for a period, and then becoming a serious businessperson. So, make partnerships, take personal loans, take money also from the state funds (if there is any), but always make sure you have a back up plan how to give back the money, in case you go broke. Do I ask too much? The bankruptcy usually occurs because of the bad husbandry, and spending money that you don't have. It takes years to earn the fortune, a long period that all of us have to pass, but not all of us have to go bankrupt to realize the essence of the good husbandry. It is not very difficult, dispose of what you have, I know it's nice to dispose of things that you don't have, but don't get in the race where you don't know how long you'll have to run to reach the goal, better enter the races where the goal is noticeable with a bare eye. That's enough for the start.)

LEARN FROM OTHERS.

(This is an advice that many people hear, but it's as if it passes trough their ears, and they do the wrong thing. I had many examples around me of how I should do some things, both in life and in business. Sometimes we get so carried away in believing we are right, that we don't see the solution hiding in front our nose. If you already have valuable persons around you, make proper use of it, learn from them and let them advise you. Besides, there are many real-life examples that could discourage you or direct you to the right address. It is necessary to have good will to listen and see what is it that other people or companies are doing, what are their experiences and how did they get where they are now. I would've stopped many drop floods if I'd wanted to listen to people around me, and stopped being a wiseacre. Fortunately, I survived the inundation, and now I find myself in the role of the man who you should listen, and whose thoughts you need to consider, so you can avoid the inundation and be smarter than I was when I first started my company.)

THE SECRET OF THE SUCCESS IS HIDING IN EVERY PERSON.

(That's right, Gentlemen, all you have to do, is to find it, and it will wake up. The road to self-knowledge is long and difficult, and in my opinion, we really don't have enough time to realize all the things we are skilled for. I support the theory that says that an average person uses barely five percent of the brain capacity, and to start using the sixth percentage he usually needs eternity. We are all made to be good and successful in a specific job, but many of us are afraid to explore the unknown because of the risk that bring the changes. Most of the people keep their job and timidly inquire (which can take years, sometimes decades) about the thing they would actually want to do. Well, my Dears, this is not how it works, this is not the way to find the secret of the success. A good start for discovering your own secret begins with things like: running towards the changes, renunciation, sacrifice, constant upgrading in business, spiritual development, courage first and fear last, etc; the result of all this efforts is the possibility to discover your deeply hidden potentials that could bring you to unthinkable heights. I know, many of you think you already know what you are doing best, you believe that nobody is better that you in that job or sport. I have one question for you: Is this all that you have to show? If the answer is YES, then thank you for answering, and if it's NO, then I say CONGRATULATIONS and good luck.)

SETTING GOALS IS A SOUL REMEDY.

(Believe it or not, sometimes I catch myself having problem in thinking over the new goals to set, while I still haven't completed the old once. Once it goes under your skin to write the goals down, and cross them out (once you've achieved them), it actually becomes a bit problematic to stop. Setting the goals doesn't mean simply writing down your wishes on a planner, anybody could do that, but writing the things that you must do. There is a big difference here, but I repeat, a very big difference. The thing that you want usually doesn't really bother you, but the thing that you must do, that's a completely different story, and this is something very bothersome. You are probably wondering, "Why would I constantly set new goals and bother myself with them, as if I don't have enough problems

in life?" My Dears, you would ask different questions if, for example, doctors would have fought six hours for your life, and you hadn't even started living it. I repeat, no one knows what tomorrow brings, so put the crucial goals in the forefront and let this kind of goals adorn your planner. Don't fool yourself thinking that you will complete them all, or that you'll accomplish everything that you decide in life. The essential thing, in these crazy times, is to be even crazier, and constantly to find new missions that will be an antidote for depression, apathy and upcoming global changes. Believe me, it helped me a lot that I didn't pay too much attention on global problems, even if they had a huge effect on my business, however my energy is continuously directed to the accomplishment of several different goals, which could change my life profoundly, or I better say my life is already changing. The ability of managing the changes by completing your own goals is one of the most efficient soul remedies. Try it; I suppose you have a soul, take some care of it.)

Just to remind you on the advices from this story:

- **GOOD HUSBANDRY PRACTICE IS CRUCIAL.**

- **LEARN FROM OTHERS.**

- **THE SECRET OF THE SUCCESS IS HIDING IN EVERY PERSON.**

- **SETTING GOALS IS A SOUL REMEDY.**

11

THE TRUTH, THE WHOLE TRUTH AND NOTHING BUT THE TRUTH

My dear Managers, Executives, Entrepreneurs, Tycoons, Politicians and Mobsters, nothing is more efficient than the truth. For the start, try to imagine that your principal business strategy is THE TRUTH. You are probably wondering what I am talking about now. When the business is based on the strategy of the truth, there are always extraordinary results. Since this book is everything but a schoolbook, I'll try to simplify. The strategy of the truth is the strategy of respecting every legal act and procedure; and even more important, that this is the strategy of fair business, without any lies, deceits, frauds, corruption and all other tricks that people use to make money. I know, I know, I know and I know, this is a very arguable subject but I won't get into philosophy, I'll just "scratch the surface".

Since my country is the best example of how things shouldn't be done, I always try to get something good from every good or bad situation, but it is very hard. Before creating my own company, I was doing many jobs and I witnessed many abnormalities. Those were both, small and big abnormalities, but it can all be considered as product of the bad times and general conditions of the society. It seemed like there was no job around me that could be completed in the proper way. Everybody doubts

everybody, everyone is afraid of being deceived (while tries to deceive others), everybody is checking back on everybody (more for the marketing, or to show the opposite side they're thorough in business; but they do it in the completely unprofessional way). At the end, they do anything to start the job (besides, they tend to express themselves incompletely, and what is unexplained in business could usually cost a lot), and end it the way they shouldn't. Naturally, not every business is like that, but here, we'll discuss those kinds of agreements, persons and their way of doing business.

Dear Friends, I am anything but naïve, but there are some things in business that I simply cannot understand, or better said 'digest'. Sometimes, I get sick of people and their attempts to be clever. Led by many different experiences, I said to myself that my future company would be based on the strategy of the truth, so Heaven help me. Naturally, at the time I didn't define it like this, but I wanted my business to be 100% transparent, to respect the legislation, and what's even more important, to make sure that all my future agreements will primary be based on mutual respect (regardless the outcome of business), transparency and business deals where both sides are satisfied. Once again we face my famous sentence, it is very difficult to stay normal, fair and correct in business, yet even today I don't know any other way.

I had a case that could make you understand the importance of the strategy of the truth. Probably, I will repeat myself, but I have to, everything that's written in this book is true, the described situations are also real life stories that I personally have lived and experienced. I'm mentioning all this, because many people will doubt, however that's their problem, but let me continue. I already spoke about my "artistic creativities", and the period of my life that I devoted to the improvement of the establishment, maintenance and promotion of intimate and high-quality relations with the opposite sex. Everyone has to pass through this and it's not something new.

Dear Friends, I believed that in business, I should be threatened by the banks, suppliers, competition, different lawyers, mobsters and usurers, etc, but I never thought I could have a problem because of a woman. Yes, yes, yes, because of a woman. I won't extend the story any more; I'll just explain the main events. After having completed the job fairly well with a person close to my family (I say fairly well since I hadn't answered to all her demands) I didn't expect the least of what was about to happen. We were having dinner and gathering the positive impressions of the completed job, but I noticed that slowly she was changing the subject and entering the

forbidden zone. I must admit: if she wasn't married and if I wasn't married to woman very close to her, I wouldn't be having second thoughts and would let the sparkling white wine do its job. Under all those circumstances, that scenario was out of the question, but that was only my opinion. She used every possible method and technique to season the well-completed job with adultery, which would actually, cost her much more that it would cost me. After my rejection, it seemed like a best solution for me, her indignation became more than obvious, and I didn't expect that reaction. Like it wasn't enough for her that I knew what she was like, and all about the guys she had cheated her husband with, unfortunately, I learned all those things after we had closed the deal (better late than never). Since I already entered the job, it was too late, but several of my acquaintances and close people had been with her, and I truly couldn't believe what kind of person she was; yet, there was nothing I could do, and it's her life anyway. Business is business, obligations are obligations, and it was my duty to fulfill them (except the last one, of course). After everything was completed, we didn't hear from each other for several months, or we didn't hear from each other ever again, but that was the least of a problem.

One morning I get a disturbing call from my father saying that several Economic Crime Inspectors were questioning our customers, clients and partners. He's also saying that they will come to our company in the short time, and we should be ready. Usually, in Serbia, when you hear about *the Economic Crime Inspector* or similar, you immediately get the pre-stroke symptoms, but I was relaxed and I said they could come whenever they wanted and the whole documentation will be in their disposal. That is the way to behave if you are a person who has nothing to hide and who does his business transparently. Half of my company paralyzed completely when they arrived, but I have to admit the Inspectors were pretty polite and professional. The Inspector explained that the reason for their coming is the criminal charges filed anonymously for tax fraud, corruption, illegal construction, money laundering (several million dollars) and another small thing that immediately engraved in my creative side of the brain. The meeting finished pretty fast, the inspectors realized that my business is transparent and they asked me at the end," . . . Do you have any idea who could resent you so much, those are pretty serious charges?" I said that I really don't know, that this is the first time that is happening, and that I am a bit shocked, but I am not surprised by their coming considering the country that we live, and the ways to run business in Serbia (they didn't have any comments, which was natural). After the meeting, I went to my

office and thought deeply about the small thing that Inspector probably shouldn't have said to me, but accidently did. Those charges were really filed anonymously, but that small thing made me realize who was hiding behind them. Naturally, if you put two and two together, and when the Inspector mentions some things known only by you and another person, the solution is more than obvious. That small thing mentioned in the criminal charges, was actually the subject of the business matter between my company and "the lady" whose flirtation I've rejected. I must admit I was a bit shocked because I couldn't believe how far the female offended vanity could go. "The lady" in question didn't know how to hurt me, so she chose an amateurish way, with amateurish criminal charges, written by half-illiterate lawyer, also amateur, and she thought it was the best solution.

The truth is, I had to dedicate one day of my life to solve the misunderstanding, but "the lady" couldn't even imagine how much she actually helped me. How did she help me? In a certain way, the Inspector's visit was a test for my company and me. We passed it with an A+. On the other hand, she doesn't even suspect that I know who had pressed the criminal charges against me (of course, after reading this book she will find out). My biggest satisfaction is exactly the fact that I know who pressed them, and I managed to transform this problem into an opportunity, and proved myself once again that I was right from the start. My dear Friends, base your business on the truth, only the truth and nothing but the truth, no matter how much it hurts and no matter how difficult it is, believe me it's easier than serving time in jail because of the criminal charges filed by the rejected "lady". Once again, I have to thank "the lady", after all, I earned a lot of money doing business with her, and she even helped me free of charge, at the end. Thank you very much, "lady".

Can you take any good advices from this story?

I'll try to help you. Here are some advices:

MEASURE TWICE, CUT ONCE.

(Now you probably say, "This boy is repeating himself. No, dear Friends, I'm not repeating myself, this considers all the things that I suppose you do thoroughly and in the right way, but I can only suppose. Every job is different and we are all very different, that's why every job demands a different behavior. It's in human nature to loosen up a bit after some time (because we think that we're doing everything like we should) and to

start overlooking the small things. Small things are always the cause of big problems. Whatever you do, measure twice and cut once, for the start it is the best way to prepare yourself. I've already mentioned the importance of the good husbandry practices, but that belongs to life philosophy, this is much smaller, this considers the everyday things, which, if you do them sloppy, might provoke the sea of drops. Oh, I know, this might sound meaningless, but if you'd analyzed more the things that you do (especially the small ones) you would realize how many omissions you have, and only by some miracle, those omissions haven't escalated to a bigger problem, which doesn't mean they won't. If I wasn't careful about the small things, I would probably be asking you now to send me a food package, while I write from prison, but fortunately, it is not so. No miracle lasts long in the business world, don't fool yourselves, put the meter in your hands, and before doing anything, measure twice and then cut, you know what I mean.)

LET THE WORST-CASE SCENARIO BE YOUR SPECIAL TREAT.

(When you come to work, invite everybody to a meeting. Declare bankruptcy, announce big time restructuring, where most of them will loose their jobs, state you are going to be arrested for tax fraud, say you don't know if you have cancer or AIDS, you'll find out later, your wife cheated on you with the gardener, and your secretary carries your twins. Since you don't want to tire out others with details, everyone should go back to their work and wait for further instructions. My dear Friends, can you imagine this scenario? Would you have the guts to try out something similar (of course to improvise)? Well, my Dears, all those things that I cited above are actually not the worst-case scenario comparing how bad things can get. The point is that in this crazy world, where neither of us is quite normal, we must deal with paranoia and different crazy tests. If you try to be normal where all the others are crazy, trust me, you won't be having a good time. I repeat, this is not a schoolbook, and I won't bother you with different business strategies, but being paranoid in these crazy times is perfectly normal and necessary. The point is to get ready for the worst-case scenario, and let it be your special treat. The devil never sleeps, and it could happen that, the moment that you put down this book, you start drowning yourself in drops of the worst-case scenario (and naturally

you are not ready for that since in those days you had some better things to do), but don't forget, those are the drops that you've created on your own.)

EVERY CRISIS IS A TEST FOR YOU AND YOUR COMPANY.

(The best way to see whether you are paranoid enough, and whether you've put the things on the right places, is in the crisis situation. The crisis situations are frequent, some are small, some are bigger, yet ever so they preoccupy our minds completely, which is quite natural, since we could lose everything, if we are not careful about their effects. There's nothing better than to be able to welcome the crisis with open arms. Most of you won't agree with me completely, as you probably think there're things that cannot be predicted, that there're things that don't depend on us, and so on . . . Actually, the things that don't depend on us are: the comet or the meteor impacts, the earthquakes, the tsunamis, other natural disasters, or the third world war. For anything else, my Dears, you can prepare yourself. Let me make a short digression, I have lived and survived through two wars in Serbia, especially when the NATO Alliance dismayed us for acting tough and smart, believe it or not, back then doing business in Serbia was much better than today. You probably wonder how it is possible. Some time before the war had begun, people knew what was about to happen and had time to prepare (as much it is possible to prepare yourself in that time of crisis). Much later, when people "apparently" had started to get involved in business, a global economic crisis began, no one expected it (or so they say), and the consequences are more than obvious. Do you see the major difference here? We had time to prepare ourselves before the bombs started to fall, and everything finished much differently than it would have if we hadn't the time to prepare, and in the second case, no one had a chance to get prepared for the global crisis, and its consequences destroyed more people than the war did. Could it be a better example: now the bombs are not falling, yet there are victims everywhere (the real impact of the global crises will be shown in the close future)? That's right, dear Friends, that's reality, so be prepared as if tomorrow bombs would start falling on your head (naturally, this sound ridiculous to many, since they hadn't lived through anything similar, but for us in Serbia it is so natural, that we almost feel uncomfortable and bizarre to be back to normal). In

this way, you will be ready for the crisis situation; be well prepared, because your survival depends on it; however, the point is—"prepare yourself", enough for the start.)

RESIST THE APPARENTY IRRESISTIBLE THINGS

(You cannot imagine how many problems I have with "the apparently" irresistible things. Actually it depends on the strength of one's character, not everyone can equally resist the temptations, better said, "the apparently" irresistible things. I accentuate, "the apparently" irresistible things. Always put in front of you your goals, as well as the goals of the job that you are about to do. When you've resolved this, take some time to think what effect a certain action could produce in the near or distant future (don't forget, the truth always comes out). Personally, the things that I could have resisted had cost me a lot in my life, it's something similar to the wrong bus that I spoke about, and the consequences could be disastrous. For example, if "the lady" in question wasn't close to my wife, and naturally if I didn't have a wife, I would definitely set a date in the more intimate place, and I don't thing we would ever have a chance to have a second sip of the champagne, but different circumstances created a different scenario. I gave a banal, but instructive example of what I have resisted, and I can say that the feeling was magnificent, but there are many different examples of temptations that you too had to face and you managed to resist. I don't know if you've already had some problems, but you certainly will have, therefore when it comes to the case similar to mine with "the lady", the message for the men is: "be careful if you put your pants down", and for the ladies: "be careful if you lift your skirts". Dear Friends, believe me, that's a dangerous luxury, and by the way, it always costs too much.)

THE TRUTH ALWAYS HURTS, BUT LET IT HURT OTHERS.

(It's a really a nice feeling when you get to see faces of the people who were convinced that you are hiding something, and when they finally realize they're wrong, but still don't believe it. You certainly had situations like this. The truth can really hurt, particularly those who have hard time dealing with the success of others (I'm talking about the envious people).

The strategy of the truth is very powerful, and there's nothing safer for you and your company, than being completely right and not having any stains in your business history. If you do have some stains, and you want to hide them, today it is almost impossible, when the truth comes out on daylight, it will hurt you a lot, as well as everyone around you. When there are no stains, the effect is doubled, first everybody suffers for not seeing any stains, and second, it hurts even more, since there's absolutely nothing he or she can do. As much as it makes you powerful, it makes them powerless. It's magnificent. It's brilliant.)

Just to remind you on the advices from this story:

- **MEASURE TWICE, CUT ONCE.**

- **LET THE WORST-CASE SCENARIO BE YOUR SPECIAL TREAT.**

- **EVERY CRISIS IS A TEST FOR YOU AND YOUR COMPANY.**

- **RESIST THE APPARENTY IRRESISTIBLE THINGS**

- **THE TRUTH ALWAYS HURTS, BUT LET IT HURT OTHERS.**

12

WHAT IS THE VALUE OF YOUR WORD

The negotiation and communication skills can be the key of the success in business negotiations, and in the same time, they could be the way to lose simply everything that you achieved until that moment. During the negotiations, it happens typically that a person, who tries to push the boundaries, does it the wrong way or that he exaggerates, and then, everybody loses.

Dear Friends, it is always possible to push the boundaries, even when they finally get set, after long negotiations, again it is possible to find space for new negotiations and further pushing. There are different ways of pushing the boundaries, but only two ways to "over cross" them, and this is what is essentially the most important. The classification is more than simple, we can sort them in visible (unprofessional) and invisible (professional) ones.

What am I talking about?

Here, it's not a question of pushing the boundaries in order to get better price or conditions for a certain product. Here it's about crossing the boundaries by people who would do anything to get out of the problem they're currently involved, and to drag someone else in that problem. The moment they decide to take that step, they already pass those boundaries,

and they are heading in the wrong direction. The visible (unprofessional) crossing of the boundaries is when you realize that somebody wants to take something from you, in the improper way, or tries to take advantage of something that you own. Usually, we notice that kind of boundaries crossing and we act on time.

What can we do about the invisible (professional) crossing of the boundaries, when only at the end you become conscious of the lies, deceit or fraud?

I could explain all this in much simpler way, but I purposely choose to use the term *crossing the boundaries,* for I think this word is the appropriate for describing those who are crossing the boundaries of decentness and proper behavior, in order to achieve their goals.

Naturally, the world is full of those people, especially of those who practice the invisible crossing of the boundaries. There are people who choose their life calling to be exactly this, the crossing of the boundaries, I'm sure that everyone had some kind of experience with persons like this. It doesn't matter in which field they operate, it always results as an illegal act, yet since those persons become so professional, sometimes it is very difficult to understand that they even have committed the legal offense. How can this be? Have they crossed the boundaries, have they done something wrong, or haven't they? Yes, my Dears, they have, but in such efficient and subtle way, that there's nothing you can do. I know, it's sad, but there's no help, sometimes-even things like this happen. I would like to mention another small detail. How would you react to a person that you know, if he passed his problem to you, and naturally, presented everything like there was no problem? How experienced are you in doing business where someone's word means much more than a contract? Naturally, in Germany, they probably have no idea what I'm talking about, but in China, they understand pretty well, what I'm saying. In some places, the contracts are formalities and in other, they're the major thing. Maybe I was raised in the wrong way, but I've learned and accepted long ago, that if I say, promise or agree to something, I have to accomplish it as well. I've accepted this philosophy also in the business, people feel it and appreciate it a lot, yet naturally, we put everything also on a paper, in form of a contract. What differentiates me from other business people is the fact that, whether there was to be a global financial crisis or not, whether the contract clauses were sustainable in certain circumstances or not, my word means much more to the people that work with me, because

they know I respect my obligations and my debts. Okay, okay, I really showed off, but I had to mention it for you to understand better the essence of the following story.

Three years ago, together with my parents I paid a visit, for no particular reason, to a family friend and his family. The man we visited was a friend of my father and a person of trust. I specially want to highlight this—person of trust—since today it's such a rare thing to find. I've accepted him and his family as my own, and we really have mutual trust and respect. During that lunch, I met his "friend" who lives abroad and does similar job like mine. To cut the story short, after a couple of days, my friend called and said that the man I've met at his house has a land suitable for constructing a residential building. He said he would like me to take it over, if I'm interested, and that this was first offered to people he and this man, know in Serbia. It sounded tempting, especially since it was offered by a man whose intentions and opinions I don't doubt. My friend wanted the best for me and for that man, and this was enough for the start. Very soon, I've met with that man and two months later, we completed the job. In the begging of the negotiations, he mentioned there was a small legal problem with the land, but he said it would be arranged already on the first court hearing. I said that made no difference and the important thing is that it is solvable, since I wanted to start the construction as soon as possible. He agreed and underlined it was only a "small problem" which would be "solved quickly".

Let me just explain myself, if it happened that my friend called and asked me to pay to that man as much as he asked, and that we'll resolve this later with contracts, I would do the same, without asking a single question or making a single remark, because I know perfectly well what my friend's word means. (Many of you probably don't understand this and possibly, you are now saying, "My dear boy, that's not the way to do business", but my Friends, those persons are rare, they exist, but they're very rare.) Three years later, I still can't catch my breath from the drops, I still have the land, but only grass and thorns grow on it, no trace of a building. The litigation is still not over and there's a big question mark on when the light will shine in the apartments of this historical building. Soon I realized that man, that business partner, has tricked me and passed me the big problem he had and left (which was not a deal, regardless the contract). When I contacted him after three years, I explained everything and said that I believe that he shouldn't act like that, yet he was falsely surprised and even more offended.

To avoid the details, at the end he told me, that it was my choice to buy that land, and that nobody forced me to do it.

That's true, my Dears, at the end, I'm a man with his problem, and he's a man with my money.

He's a good example for the people who don't hold on to their words, who have no scruples or fear. Without second thoughts, he made a deal with me, he used the friendship with my trust person, took the money and left me with the problem, which, dear Friends, I still haven't solved. Would you pass to anyone a nicely wrapped problem? It was not a small problem, it was a big one and it wasn't solved quickly, and no one knows when it will be. That kind of deal is not to be made even with an enemy, let alone with the man who's your friend's best friend. You cannot image the reaction of my friend who, I repeat, wished the best to all of us. When he heard the story, he couldn't sleep for days and he felt extremely responsible. I said that he was not to feel any responsibilities since I know that he wished only the best for everyone, and that he had no bad intentions, that in the way, he was also deceived.

You say something today, and then at the end, it appears that your word is worth nothing, because your actions speak more about your intentions. If it were for an enemy, you would know he's your enemy, and you'd know what to expect, but when your friend becomes your enemy, that's twice as worse, don't ever doubt it and try not to put yourself in this kind of situation. I promise myself, in spite of all the problems that have emerged, and in spite of the contract clauses, I will construct that building, and that I'll fix everything that needs to be fixed. Sometimes you can make a contract where everything is crystal clear and to face a disaster, and there are times when it's enough to have a good agreement, and a contract only as formality, to complete all the set goals in the best possible way and to obtain the highest profits. That's the way it goes, I had several similar cases but with people who respect what they say, and who stand still behind their words. Are you a kind of person who stands still behind his words, or you just think you are? If you are, my doors and the doors of the whole world are wide open for doing business with you, but if you just think that you are like that, in that case you'll open one or two doors, but after that you won't be opening other doors ever again.

Can you take any good advices from this story?

I'll try to help you. Here are some advices:

ALWAYS PUSH, BUT NEVER CROSS THE BOUNDARIES.

(Try to decide on which side you will lead your life and your business. I'm a fan of pushing the boundaries to the maximum, but not of crossing them. Whatever you decide to do, try doing it as good as possible, there's only one thing in this story that you should pay special attention. A person, who pushes the boundaries in business, stays in business, a person who crosses the boundaries in business, crosses also the boundaries in every segment of his life, and at the end, his chances of staying in business become miserable, and all the doors of the world of business remain closed, forever. This is why it's important to push the boundaries carefully, to watch where you are heading, and where you are stopping.)

ALL THAT GLITTERS IS NOT GOLD.

(My Dears, I know that after a battle, everyone is a general, but from the start, I had small doubts about the man who currently enjoys my money, while I'm suffocating in the problem that was previously his and currently is mine. I couldn't be happier! In spite of my suspicions, I still considered him in the friendly way, because, maybe in a way, I wanted that man to be equally good as my friend. It's nice to have whishes but let's face the reality. That person was an illusion of something good and truthful (he glittered like gold, but only for a moment) and it was enough for me to swallow the hook. There are many similar people around you, and you better believe your instinct when it implies even a grain of doubt for a certain job or a specific person, don't ever take it too lightly. Everybody relaxes at some point, but try to find some time to investigate. We all earn our money with difficulty (almost all), it doesn't matter how much you would lose from a certain job, just let this lost be a product of a bad marketing, tough competition or similar, don't let that lost be a consequence of a fraud or deceit, for it hurts much more than the money that you lose. There are times when we need to open our eyes a bit more widely than usual, because it can happen that one's person gold glitter makes the person next to him shine as well, but there's a significant difference between those two persons, one is a true gold, while the other isn't even gild, it's only cheap old iron.

Some people realize it on time; while others, like me, lose a lot. No worries, if you forgot even for a moment other examples like this, at least, this story reminded you not to make my mistake, which is the essence of this book.)

PUT ALL YOUR CARDS ON THE TABLE.

(I know that it can be very difficult, especially since you would like to keep secret about one unimportant detail, which you don't believe could provoke a big problem. STOP IT, STOP IT and STOP IT! This will be a short advice. Details are things that provoke huge fights, wars, crisis situations, etc, which speaks about their importance. Expose everything that you have, naturally, with the help of all your manager—leader—communication skills, try to make it look right, but, my Dears, it is necessary that you put all your cards on the table. What you don't pay today, you'll pay tomorrow; don't leave things unspoken, because they'll have to be spoken someday; don't try to hide things; someday they'll have to be discovered. If you find this difficult, and you think I'm wrong, then I must express my greatest regrets, because we might see each other in business for another day, month, or year, and then we certainly won't see each other again. That's the way it is, you know it, and those who don't show all their cards know it as well, but ok, they believe that puts them in a rank of "big business players and experts". They don't really care what people like me have to say, but this is why we are more, and it's good that we are eating the main course, and they have only the crumbs. I wish them good appetite.)

EVERY AGREEMENT OR CONTRACT SHOULD BE TAKEN WITH CAUTION.

(This is an extension of the advice *All that glitters is not gold*. Here is what it's all about. My friend wanted the best for everyone, but it turns out the job wasn't done correctly, and there are large consequences. He never had bad intentions yet the results remain the same. In spite of the fact that someone is a very good friend of yours, dear Friends, that doesn't mean that he could not be deceived or tricked; on the contrary, he could easily be the missing link chain for someone wanting to seize you, without even realizing it. This is exactly what happened in this case, it's just that I wasn't

careful, and I entered the job doughtily, without any caution. Always enter a job with caution, especially when it's a friend's recommendation, because when there are no recommendations, you find it natural to analyze all the details and check everything; also when there is a recommendation, be prudent and spare some time to check out the things. You won't be doing this in order to check out your friend, but to possibly open your friend's eyes, if it happens that you feel the deception or betrayal. I hope that I managed to help my friend after everything that had happen to me, and that he took the lesson. Some people take their lesson with big losses, like me, so slow down for a moment and don't repeat my mistakes, yet you should arm yourself with caution—and off to the battle.)

Just to remind you on the advices from this story:

- **ALWAYS PUSH, BUT NEVER CROSS THE BOUNDARIES**

- **ALL THAT GLITTERS IS NOT GOLD.**

- **PUT ALL YOUR CARDS ON THE TABLE.**

- **EVERY AGREEMENT OR CONTRACT SHOULD BE TAKEN WITH CAUTION.**

13

LEARN TO SAY NO

Lots of authors of books similar to this one (at least roughly similar) speak about different methods and techniques for realizing when is the moment that you have to stop, and which are the situations where you firmly have to say NO. Without a doubt, there are good advices how to avoid the sea of drops with the simple answer: NO, NO, and NO. Naturally, until now, in most of the cases I use to say YES, when I had to say firmly NO.

What is it that makes us block out in certain moments, and makes us say *yes*?

I've made countless mistakes and failures because I was making decisions too hasty, even about the details, which, I repeat, can grow to disaster. As time was passing, I was becoming more experienced in negotiating, and the frequent YES was slowly, but surely, stopping to be so frequent. I must mention that young people face much trouble in the negotiations, and in managing the company in general. Over 90% of people weren't taking me seriously, they didn't even want to talk to some kid, and those who did spare some time, after all, were looking how to sell their trading tricks and make as much money as possible. Many did earn much more than what they deserved, but I earned even more, so it's not even important

anymore. For a short period, but I put the accent on "short", in Serbia the construction business was blooming. There were new buildings arising in every corner, the demand was huge, and the offer not so enviable, which made the prices so high to the point that that we practically reached Paris and London, considering the value of the gross national income. At that time, I was completing one building and starting up two more. The sales were great, the profit was fantastic, but naturally, every nice thing has to end, and so this ended very quickly. The global financial crises knocked on the door and did its way, which stopped our course of growing rich. Naturally, the life goes on and the business must follow as well. In the time of crises, I earned invaluable experience, and now I know very well what I'm looking for, when I analyze a certain land.

One of my agents came with a story that there's a very good land, on a fabulous location, and that the conditions are not so rigorous. I won't get into the details, but when you get whipped so hard by the crises, that you almost could feel the taste of bankruptcy, then, you know very well what to do. The land prices were unreal because the owners were still living in the time before the crises. On the other hand, the land was not only good, it was perfect, everything that I was looking for I had on that location; it was a big investment, but also a big profit. It is incredible how much I wanted this land, I spent days analyzing and all the indices showed that the location was profitable; however, the owners were asking too much considering the current times. The negotiations lasted over two months and finally came the last meeting. The meeting had started, and it was only left to agree about some "details" so that the lawyers could start doing their job. My company really needed that job, however, in one moment I started to see images from the time of crises when I had so many problems. I really don't know why, I wasn't thinking about it, I was excited to complete finally the job. I was almost not present at the meeting, but when I came back to reality, I interrupted the people who were talking and declared the following, "Dear Gentlemen, these business negotiations last pretty long, finally we are close to make an agreement, but we are only close. I must apologize, I know that you were expecting the signing of the contract today, but I need more time." Since he understood that we really wanted that land, one of the owners said, "Sir, we have waited for a long time, you are not the only company who wants our land, if you want to sign, now is your chance, and if you don't, you want have that chance anymore." What a good trading trick! My answer was short: "Gentlemen, this meeting is over, my final answer for this location is NO, thank you for your time".

Everyone in the meeting room was completely shocked, after all, we were the ones who were chasing the owners to buy that land, we were the initiators of the job, but I didn't want to be blackmailed, not this time. After they've left, I got a bunch of negative critics, but that was my final decision. You cannot imagine how good I felt, it was as if I lost a heavy burden, which I was carrying on my back. In the last moment, during that meeting, I realized that if I had signed the contract, I would've put a huge burden on my back. Despite the fact that the business seemed profitable in that moment (in spite of all analyzes), I had a dose of suspicion (he who has been bitten by a snake is afraid of an eel). The owners of that land still cannot sell the property, and after all, it turned out that my decision was good. Several times, they tried to restart the negotiations with us, but they always came across a polite NO. Several months later, the investments completely stopped, the real estate market experienced an outrageous collapse and a large number of companies simply disappeared. I would have disappeared with them if I'd said YES. Sometimes, it's very difficult to say NO, but the feeling is magnificent, when you learn to say it the right time and manage to be right in the end. It's fantastic.

Can you take any good advices from this story?

I'll try to help you. Here are some advices:

BEFORE YOU MAKE ANY DECISION—SLEEP ON IT.

(Until not so long ago, I was advising people that some decisions require to be slept on. When I say decisions, I don't mean buying tomatoes and potatoes, I mean the decisions that can have a large influence on the development of your company, and coincidently on your life. Many of us believe that the decisions won't have great importance and they're not crucial for the survival of the company, so we make them easily. I admitted to many people who I've advised previously, that I was wrong when I was saying that "*certain* decisions", instead it is necessary that "*every* decision has to be slept on". My Dears, I already said that devil never sleeps, and that in most of the cases he's hiding in small things. Take seriously every decision making, whether it's about hiring a new employee or buying a new car; and if someone can't wait, while your decision is on thin ice, and you didn't have a chance to think it trough, firmly say NO and go on. It's a very powerful feeling.)

I'M JUST A PASSENGER;
NEVER EVEN SAW THE CAPTAIN.

(This refers to the global economy situation. I don't want to get any deeper in this subject, even though I have so much material about who actually rules our destiny, that I could write a very big book, here I will just "scratch the surface", as I like to say. My Dears, almost nobody could predict the global financial crises (except those who actually created it, but hush, we won't talk about it), and people were just entering new projects without having second thoughts. The rare individuals who practice the good husbandry had a backup plan, and the arrival of the crises didn't damage them a great deal, but the others suffered a lot. I'll be short and clear; you need to understand the crucial thing in managing the company; it refers to the fact that neither you or I are navigating this ship, we are only passengers, while the big ones, in the best-case scenario, are only the lowest crew rank. As far as the navigating elite, you can make your own conclusions. In this case, they're having a nice lunch, while the most of us get only the crumbs. It's simple, that's how the system works, and you need to accept it. When you accept it, and when you are aware of it, which is even more important than accepting it, then you'll always know that as soon as tomorrow you could have a shipwreck. My dears, if you know all this, I won't doubt the decisions you'll make, there's only one path so walk on it carefully.

BLACKMAILING IN BUSINESS MEANS NO
COURAGE; IT MEANS FEAR.

(The blackmail can be successful, or it can fail, but if you ever find yourself in a situation similar to the one I described above, please just stop for a moment and take a deep breath. Most of the people who decide to use this kind of extortion usually feel fear, fear of losing you, they don't currently have a second choice, or they can't wait any longer. That's their weakness, don't let it be yours, so remain indifferent to the blackmail attempts, stick to your conditions and simply say NO. I know it's hard, because you're afraid of losing a brilliant opportunity. Consider all the given circumstances, and put yourself in the position of the person you are negotiating with, only this time, you blackmail them. You cannot imagine what their reaction will be, you won't be surprised, you'll be stunned, nobody likes to be blackmailed,

and few would expect it from a company in situation like that; especially since the company was the initiator of the business, and it wasn't supposed to make too much noise. Therefore, don't get involved in blackmails, instead make your decisions sensibly, that will make a much better reputation than blackmailing. Wise decisions travel fast. Think about it.)

NEVER COME BACK TO PAST.

(Whenever I got back together with an ex girlfriend (I never did with the ex wives), it was good as long as the momentary chemical explosion lasted (you know what I mean)—and that was it. After that, the both sides (in the best case, the both sides) realize that's not it anymore, and they should go on and find a better opportunity. Naturally, during the separation, in most of the cases, both sides don't speak too nicely of each other, and they especially underline that there are no chances for their reconciliation. What a stupid thing to do and I did it many times. It says a lot about the person (come on, don't you stick to your word, don't you have a character, any self-respect or something?). I said to myself hundred times not to think about satisfying my needs in those situations, but to think with the creative side of the brain. My Dears, you've all been in those situations, and you've all made mistakes, lucky for me I learned that lesson long ago, and those things don't happen anymore. What does this have to do with the business and the story I told before? Actually, it has a lot. If you've already made a decision not to buy something, or not to sign or sell, then it's final, don't turn back, and just go on. Imagine if I called back the owners of the land, that I previously walked out politely from my office (who wanted to lynch me in that moment). Imagine if I told them that I've thought it over and realized that I over did it, that I had been under stress the other day, and that I would like to meet with them in order to see how we could renew the negotiations. From that moment, you already started to drown in drops and you didn't even realize it. They would be under the impression that now you are even more interested, that you are an unstable person, that you don't have any better land offers or other options. Under all the mentioned circumstances, they would try to change the conditions, and to ask for more money for that land, since they've seen that you're truly pushing it, and your weakness is revealed. That's why, my Dears, don't look back, just go on; and try to remember how it feels, when you realize that you've got back together with your ex girlfriend, only for the sake of getting lade,

and you didn't even realize it. You're drowning in drops, you're spending your time, as well as hers, you're making a fool of yourself, and all that just for getting lade, in other words, to go back to past and make a mistake. So, forget about the past, just think about new opportunities—and look forward.)

THERE'S ALWAYS A BETTER CHANCE, JUST SAY, "NO".

(I know that after this story you have only one question that is bothering you: "What if that was the best chance ever and I'll never get a chance like this again?" Dear Friends, it's not as if we are facing a danger of comet crash and you didn't managed to get on board of the spaceship to save yourself. Don't panic for no reason, there are much more chances than you think, even if you could live three lives you wouldn't be able to spend them. So, we've solved that, and I'm saying this because similar things had happen to me in real life (not with women, but with the company). I know one must have big guts in certain moments, but nothing is definitive and certain but the death, but that's another topic; so come to your senses and after each NO, say: "there's always a better chance" and you won't believe how quickly it will come true.)

Just to remind you on the advices from this story:

- **BEFORE YOU MAKE ANY DECISION—SLEEP ON IT.**

- **I'M JUST A PASSENGER; NEVER EVEN SAW THE CAPTAIN.**

- **BLACKMAILING IN BUSINESS MEANS NO COURAGE; IT MEANS FEAR.**

- **NEVER COME BACK TO PAST.**

- **THERE'S ALWAYS A BETTER CHANCE, JUST SAY, "NO".**

14

ARE YOU A SHOWMAN OR
AN OBSERVER?

My Dears, we've reached the story we all have lived many times, and many of us have reacted the same way in certain moments. What kind of situations is it about? I'm talking about different celebrations, festivities, birthdays, private parties, company parties (very important), etc. We all like to have good time, and I believe many of you sing in the shower and dance in front of the mirror, but what's with that singing and dancing in the places where you're supposed to do it? Are you one of those people who repress their need to dance, sing (or should I say go crazy? Sometimes, of course) and just watch the others, or the party is simply not a party without you? I know that sometimes, it's very difficult to take the step and simply go to the dance floor, especially when everybody is standing and watching you. Have you ever been in a similar "awkward situation"? Do you care about the strange looks, while you're having fun? Do those looks affect you to the point that you feel uncomfortable, even as an observer?

I could still ask many more questions, but they all lead to the same answers, and it is—are you a showman or an observer? I know, you're probably saying now, I'm neither a showman nor an observer, even so I know how to enjoy myself, as much as it suits me. Well my Dears, everything

would be just fine, if I would actually believe you. There's one thing I know for sure, you'll never get back all the things that you've missed that evening, and all this for hesitating or worrying about the strange looks. I'm telling you all this because of the sentence said by an unknown person, that got engraved deep in my memory, and which says a lot.

I always liked to sing, dance and have as much fun as possible. I like to make the best of the evening, and I always do. It would never be that way if I hadn't played the major part, and did everything I could so that my Friends and I would have great time. I simply cannot stand the observers when it's about having fun, I know that everybody would like to jump in and dance while their favorite song is playing, but they have inner barriers that don't allow them to set free. Music is an incredible motivator, if it didn't exist, I don't know if I would ever work out so much, but let me continue.

During my artistic creations, as I like to call it (I already mentioned it before), I always tried to get the best out of the party, and out of the people. It's an incredible feeling when you can move someone, and finally see what kind of person he is when he loosens up and starts enjoying the evening. It's very hard but I always succeed. Why is it so important? Am I trying to liberate you from your complexes or your mental brakes? Well no, my Dears, you'll do it on your own in time, that's not something difficult, I just want to make you realize the way that other people see your behavior when you're partying, and how it can reflect on your job. After a short brake, I organized a small company party in a nightclub, where I invited all the employees and several friends from the outside. I devoted as much as an hour for all the preparations (an experienced person doesn't need more time), so that we could have as much fun as possible. I tried hard to wake up the sleepy ones, and I can proudly say that even the shiest ones hit the floor. I was very glad about it, and in spite of the problems, I had these days, I tried to emit positive energy, so that everybody would feel positive. It was long past midnight and I was dancing with a friend, a girl approached, politely apologized, and said, "It's more than obvious who's pushing all the strings here, sorry once again, bye!" I greeted her politely and looked at her a bit oddly, because in that moment I didn't quite realize what she wanted to say, but those words engraved deeply in the, naturally, creative side of my brain.

The next day I thought about that sentence and I understood its meaning. She was not coming on to me, I got that quickly, but she was probably watching the whole group from the side, and she gave her

comment. She took the liberty to approach me and to say what she had noticed. We didn't know each other, and there was no reason for her to approach me, but she did it anyway and said how she felt. I don't know what brought her to say that, probably she saw how much effort I had invested to wake those sleeping beauties, and maybe just that inspired her to state simply her opinion. I really don't know what her motivation was, but she noticed that someone was sticking out in the crowd, standing out with the positive energy, which affected other people as well. I knew that I could make quite an impression on others because I really try hard, but I never paid too much attention on how the rest of the people would react. Anyhow, I found it out in a very nice way.

Can you take any good advices from this story?

I'll try to help you. Here are some advices:

GET THE MOST OF EACH SITUATION.

(My dear Friends, life is too short to waste time on hesitation, mental barriers or complexes. Put all this aside, direct your energy in the right way, and take the most of each situation. It doesn't matter if it's about having fun or doing business. How many times did you regret for not saying something at the meeting with the manager, and you really wanted to, how many times did you want to say your opinion, but you put it off for the next time? There's no next time, my Dears, there's only today, and today's opportunity, tomorrow is another day but with different opportunities, don't forget it. No one will misunderstand you if you want to get the most of a situation to achieve something positive. Everyone welcomes it as one of the characteristics of the people who always move forward, of those people who stand out in the crowd; some call them leaders, but they're far from being observers.)

BE THE FIRST ONE TO DANCE.

(This is very important and you cannot believe how much effect it can have in business, when people know that you don't have any barriers, and you'll always be the first to dance. Naturally, it is very important how you dance in business, but some people never even get to the dance floor. It's necessary that you become an initiator, a person who starts every action

and a person who completes every action in the way that leaves everybody breathless. Every effort pays out, I've already mentioned it before, and it's important to lift your effort to the next level, to the level where you lead the dance. Tango is a dance for two, but the one who looks powerful is the one who's leading the dance. Make the first step, and be the first one to dance, be the one who's leading the dance, the results will be fabulous. Try it out.)

EMIT THE POSITIVE ENERGY.

(This is a condition of all conditions. If you emit negative energy, first you do no good to yourself, not to mention the others. I always say to my employees that they couldn't even dream of how many problems I have, and what are all the things that I do to survive, but I leave all the negative energy at the company's door, and the positive thinking is my only option. Sometimes it's quite difficult to find the way of the positive energy; we are living in extremely crazy times. For the start, make yourself extremely crazy (in a positive way, of course), and don't let someone's negative craziness infect you with the negative energy. If you are crazier than the others are, or if you always have answers or actions to their remarks, that will leave them speechless and even breathless, then, my Dears, you are the producer of the positive energy. And, do you know why? It's because you've beaten all the negative remarks, and this will make you happy; and the product of that happiness will be the positive energy, which you'll use to infect the others. Let them all wonder how it's possible that you're always in a good mood (even if you're not, of course), and you always glow with positive energy; at least their jealousy will make them open up their eyes and realize the world is filled with different colors. That attitude will make you have smaller oscillations in your business problems, and bigger oscillations regarding your progress (to the top, naturally), at least that's what has happened to me, and that will happen to you too, if you just think positive, the result will be positive as well.)

ALWAYS BE NOTICED.

(I don't want to give you lessons about the importance of the looks, and how much it means to you, and to your company. We're living in the most

sophisticated era since there's humanity; people earn millions through their image, for they know what it means to be noticed. I don't want to speak here about famous persons, but about us, common people, who have to do everything to stand out in the crowd, and not to be eaten by sharks. Be noticed, but in the right way. Don't hang out in fashionable cafés or clubs rather plan carefully your artistic creativity. I repeat, since you're already trying, better directing your energy in the right way. The energy, directed carefully is like a light in a dark, it's almost impossible to be unnoticed. Don't try to impress the others, there's no need for that, rather impress yourself, achieve what you really want, realize the positive thoughts, infect the ones around you with your positive energy, and the results can be magnificent; for the start, someone will come to you and say, "It's more than obvious who's pushing all the strings here." That's enough for the start; you're on the right path.)

Just to remind you on the advices from this story:

- **GET THE MOST OF EACH SITUATION**

- **BE THE FIRST ONE TO DANCE.**

- **EMIT THE POSITIVE ENERGY.**

- **ALWAYS BE NOTICED.**

15

DO NOT SCORN A WEAK CUB. HE MAY BECOME THE BRUTAL TIGER.

The title of this story is an old Mongolian proverb that I read before the beginning of the movie about the life of the great Mongolian conqueror, Temudjin-Genghis Khan. This proverb perfectly describes his life, as well as the life of all those who use their persistence, patience and wise decisions, to accomplish their life goals. Many of us have to start from the bottom, while others have a good business foundation that they inherited from their parents or family. I know, fortune to one is mother, to another is stepmother. Imagine a person who had a good business foundation left from his parents, and because of his rebel nature, he has rejected everything and has started from the bottom. You already recognize the person—it's me, of course.

We are all very different, and we all have different opinions of how life should be lived. For the fighters, like us, there's only one road, and it's the road to victory. Genghis Khan didn't want to know the meaning of the word defeat, and above all, he believed in achieving his goals. He became the biggest threat when people noticed the new tiger among them. Even today, nothing has changed.

Read the following lines carefully, they could turn out very helpful. Since I started my own company, I've passed through various stages of the business life cycle, from birth to death. When my company was born, saying I was unnoticeable among the tigers, is too mild, I was actually invisible. Big tigers walk proudly through society, some are good, some are evil, but they all enjoy the mighty predator status, and they're not to joke with. I've always considered myself being the successor of the big tiger (my father), and that's why in a certain way, I always had to carry the burden of his fame, in both sports and business.

This means that in the start I was a cub, which was kicked, mocked, underestimated, disregarded, but sometimes also complimented. The positive criticism and the occasional jobs are what kept me alive, at least until I matured enough. On my short journey, I was injured many times, but to my fortune, all the wounds healed well, and in those places, the skin is now much thicker and is impossible to cut it through.

Since the big tigers are always busy, and have better things to do than to watch other animals, especially weaker tigers, often it happens that they pay no attention to the rumors about the young tigers' individual successes, by saying they don't care at all, and that it means nothing to them. I cannot say that all the tigers are like that, but most of them truly are. Many years have passed, and a small tiger entered the world of the big ones; indeed, he entered through the small door but he was still noticed. The young tiger, or should I say, my company under my leadership, started to have more serious jobs and to collect more serious profit, and as soon as you start occupying the part of the territory, immediately you become noticed and become a threat. I see things a bit differently, I see other tigers as opportunities, I'm not afraid of them; I try to be part of the jungle, where I won't be attacking their prey, I won't be sharing it with them, but they can never even think about approaching my prey, because they know that this would cause a brutal fight. Stronger the tigers—the jungle will be stronger, only the battle of knowledge and expertise would be able to determine who would gather more fruits and would become even stronger.

Precisely those mighty tigers, who were disparaging me and treating me like a squirrel, and not like a tiger, were the ones who were the most surprised with my success, both in business and in private life. Only then, you realize, by their comments and the look in their face, that they respect you now, because they actually fear you, and they're so afraid of your success that there's nothing smart they could say. It happened to me personally, and it's a wonderful feeling. A certain number of tigers know my way of

doing business, and know what path I take to accomplish my goals. My path is not a secret, in this book you can come to know me even better, but there's a big truth in this whole story, and that is the fact even if you know my reflections, my path is very difficult, and only a few tigers remain on it. I don't know for any other path, but I know that I'm still growing, and I know that I'm being noticed, and I know that it bothers the other tigers, and I know that those who are scared are those who were not good to me, and I know they fear my decisions. However, you and I, we can only send one message to tigers around us, that we are the tigers of the next generation, our instincts are more perceptive than yours, our reflexes are faster that yours, our skin is thicker and our claws are sharper than yours are. We are saying all this just to make you erase forever the stereotypes that you have about the power, and to make you remember the sentence: "Do not scorn a weak cub. He may become the brutal tiger."

Can you take any good advices from this story?

I'll try to help you. Here are some advices:

BECOME A TIGER, LIVE LIKE ONE AND DIE LIKE ONE.

(I've already mentioned something similar (but only similar) when I said that, if once you are a fighter, you'll always be a fighter. Being a fighter is only one of the ways to survive, while being a tiger is a surviving philosophy. It takes a lot of effort, patience, wise decisions, and luck to pass all the stages of tiger's life. Regardless your occupation, it takes a lot of courage to decide to walk through life as a tiger, every job and every profession have their tigers. The moment that you became a tiger, it means that you start seriously doing business, your goal is to enter the world of big tigers, and then it is necessary that you survive through the maturing period. This is the first problem, and this is where many of you disappear. Don't allow yourself to fall for small things. Million times, they tried to trick me into making a false step, but fortunately, I didn't take out the claws, since I knew that I would accomplish my goals in a different way, and not by letting being provoked. When you've grown into a tiger that starts strutting in society, then you must always have on your mind the brutal law of surviving in jungle, and you must particularly remember the period when you were a growing young tiger. This world is unpredictable, there's danger on every corner, that's why the life of the tiger is hard, because he knows there's

death waiting for him on every corner, and that there's no time to relax. You know pretty well that the tiger is a predator that frightens everybody, but it's up to you to make everyone realize, with your competence, knowledge and wise decisions, that it takes a lot to cut through your skin and cause a deathblow. The tigers are especially afraid of the successes of the others and they really hate it. When you finally create the balance in the tigers' world, and when you become one of the big ones, you'll know how to accomplish your goals, and who knows, since you got that far, you might even give me some useful advice. You never know.

TREAT OTHERS AS YOU TREAT YOURSELF.

(My Dears, don't burn the bridges behind you only because of your complexes, pride or because you think it's the best way to teach someone a lesson. You know very well how the children remember everything, we've all been through that, and that's one big truth. I have some childhood memories deeply engraved in my mind and it's impossible to forget them. I already mentioned how I hate the injustice, and how I cannot stand any kind of abuse. Many of us, the tigers, don't treat the young tigers as correctly as we should. Don't forget that, even the young tigers have their opinions, their wishes, their thoughts and hopes, that's not the privilege of the grown ups. It is very important how you treat the young tigers and other animals, because in the near future you could become their prey. Express your respect to everyone, it's the least that you can do, and this way your bridges will stand steel and this would be remembered, and when the young tigers' time comes, you will only have allies and never opponents.)

TIGERS ARE ONLY A PART OF THE JUNGLE.

(That's right, my dear Tigers, I must disappoint you, we are only a part of the jungle, and actually, things work that way, that whether we like it or not, whether we want it or not, we need to communicate and cooperate with other animal species, who represent the rest of our crazy and beautiful jungle. Oh yes, we are not alone. The jungle is full of different animal species, where each one has its own place and its own role in the jungle. My dear Tigers, not everyone are tigers, but all the tigers depend on other animals, and other animals demand a special approach and collaboration so

they will accomplish what you wish. Therefore it's very important to build carefully and wisely the relations with other animals, because you mustn't forget that they can all do without you, but you cannot do without them. Just to know who is indispensable if you want to build and keep your small empire in the huge jungle, you need to know who is essential for you.)

THE TIGERS HAVE EVOLVED.

(I have a feeling that the big players—the tigers, are bigger than ever. I am aware of the fact that we live in the most sophisticated era since there's humanity, but do you ever get simply excited by the big strategies, ideas or achievements of certain individuals? They keep on pleasantly surprising me, and they're becoming all more frequent. The cruel capitalism has one magnificent quality, which is the development of science and knowledge. In everyday competitions human brains are tested to the final limits of endurance of the body (still I believe that even the biggest minds use only small percentage of their brain possibilities), and as result we get some amazing strategies, products, theories, etc. Dear Gentlemen, the biggest stimulation for that is the big tigers' brutal chase of the profit; they invest billions in the development of the knowledge so that the humanity could climb one more step. It's simple, it's humane and naturally, it's profitable.

Just to remind you on the advices from this story:

- **BECOME A TIGER, LIVE LIKE ONE AND DIE LIKE ONE.**

- **TREAT OTHERS AS YOU TREAT YOURSELF.**

- **TIGERS ARE ONLY A PART OF THE JUNGLE.**

- **THE TIGERS HAVE EVOLVED.**

16

AND AFTER ME—AGAIN ME

I like to say that I wish all my employees were thinking the way I'm thinking. Very smart, isn't it? Yes, it is. All the employers, including me, primary try to reach efficiently the conscience of their employees, to make them realize, at least for a moment, the very essence of the set goals, and understand what their employer really wants. Sometimes I think it's more difficult to reach the minds of the employees than to the minds of the clients and customers. Weird, isn't it? The least I like to do is waste someone's time.

How do you feel about wasting your time?

I consider it being a useless process, especially when the employees do it. How do they do it? Not all the employees are the same, some waste time, others use tricks to avoid working, thirds invent meetings, and some do everything to complete their job as efficiently as possible. Those employees, who don't listen properly, typically waste your time, and as a result, they make series of omissions in the accomplishment of the set goals. Those omissions demand our time again, and then, when you realize it's not your mistake, but the employee has wondered off, then some serious problems appear. You start to realize that all the meetings with that person were futile, and that he doesn't respect your time. I know that many people don't think

this way, but if that person was sitting in vain in your office, and he heard only every third word, then he was wasting his time, and when someone doesn't respect himself and his own time, how can he respect you and your time? Naturally, sooner or later, these kinds of employees emerge to the surface, especially in small companies. What can I say, these days it's very difficult to find a worker who fulfills his obligations exactly as you want him to, and when there's a problem he solves it quickly and efficiently, without crying for help. Did you ever think about cloning yourself? I constantly think about that option.

I'm repeating, we are all different and we all have different values. Each company has workers who are efficient, those who are less efficient, and those who are completely inefficient; but each company has its own way of building the relations between the staff, but I don't want to go down to that. My Dears, it doesn't matter what is your position in the company, and it doesn't matter if you are a shopkeeper or a General Manager, what matters is the way that you perform your job. It's necessary that you do magnificently the job that you're assigned to, to the point that you even envy yourself for the performance. Let me say it the simplest possible way: you must work as if it was your own company. I know now, many would say, me too I do my best, what do you want, you want me to give my life for the company. My Dears, you can do your best and actually do nothing, because you don't do it properly. That's why it is very important in which way you complete your duties, and how efficient you are in it. What distinguishes certain employee from the others is precisely his way of working and handling his obligations. It is very important to recognize people with potentials, people with leadership skills, the charismatic ones, simply those who stand out in the crowd. It's precisely in that crowd, my Dears, that your clones are hiding.

Are you like that, do you stand out in the crowd, could you take over the leadership of the company?

First, those people do their job remarkably; they solve efficiently the problems and follow carefully your every move, not to mention the words. That means that those individuals are devoted, ready to work and advance, they are ready to learn more and improve themselves further, ready for the changes.

Fortunately for me, I recognized a person who firmly heads to a high position in my company. One day, I called him in my office and we had a long conversation; I told him that I've noticed his qualities, and that he should continue the good work. I said that I'm always at his disposal,

and that it's necessary to work much more to reach the stars; I also said that it's going to be very difficult for him, that I'll be one of his biggest problems at work, but that he was on the right path. He works all more with me now; it's incredible how much he resembles me in certain things (which is not that good, but I also tell him that), he's absolutely devoted to his obligations, he completes his tasks creatively and in short terms. It's very important that the two-way communication helped us to reach each other's conscience, and to put things in the way it suits us both. He accepts really well all the remarks regarding the building of his leadership skills and his work performance. At the end of a certain meeting, where he made a very good impression on everyone, quite self-confidently (probably overwhelmed with his performance) he said, "Your stories and advices mean a lot to me, especially the stories about the mistakes that you've made; for the start, my strategy is not to make the same mistakes that you did. Actually, I could say that it's going pretty well, both at work and in private life". To that I answered, "It is very good that you follow that path. I don't know if I'd be here today, if I have been guided by the experiences of other people, still I'm here because of my mistakes, I wish you become much better and much more successful than me, but my mistakes won't be enough for that, you're going to have to make some of your own, too." He understood that I wish him the best, and that's why he attempts to be all better and more efficient. Sometimes, when I look behind, or when I look sideways to his work, with the smile on my face, I say, "Great, even after me—again me".

Can you take any good advices from this story?

I'll try to help you. Here are some advices:

LEARN TO LISTEN

(Are you a good listener? How often do you interrupt the person who's speaking? What is your body language while you're listening? There are much more questions that partially reveal the kind of listener you are, but I think you best know it yourself. I've already mentioned that I'm not like most of the authors who name different "scientifically proved" techniques of how to become a good listener. I personally think that I'm not the world's best listener, but I continuously improve myself in that sense. I use to interrupt people constantly when they were talking, because I couldn't stand to listen to all the stupidities they were saying. There were times

they were not saying stupidities, yet, I was not patient enough to listen until they would finish, and I considered myself too smart for that. You need to restrain your nature, to be calm and patient, regardless the meeting difficulty, and you must listen carefully to the other person. Amazingly, people tend to say much more than they want to, if only you let them. If I knew it before, I would never interrupt my employees when they were talking, not even when they'd stop for a while to remember something, I would always let them finish their thought. In that way I would hear more, I would give better advices and make better decisions. It is very important what I'm saying here; I had a lot of damage because I didn't know how to listen, and sometimes I didn't want to, which is even worse. Practicing, you'll best learn how to listen to others, but always remember that they will say at least one more word than they wanted to, just because your listening put them in that position. This is not speculating, this is paying respect; everyone values that, and it could mean a lot to you.)

LEARN TO MAKE OTHERS LISTEN TO YOU.

(This is a different story. To be honest, you must know both: to listen and to be listened to; one doesn't go without the other. I caught myself talking for months, individuals from my company pretended to listen, but they didn't hear much. For that, my Dears, I only blame myself for not noticing it. I was rushing things, and I was chasing the profit, while they were chasing the end of the month because of the payday. Every conversation demands time. The way that you made your speech and sent the message, determines the results that you can anticipate. Besides, don't expect others to listen, if you don't listen yourself to what you are saying. Good oratory is tightly connected to the charisma. It takes many things to become a good orator, but to make ourselves clear, we're not talking here, for example, about rhetoric skills that a president of the USA needs, but I'm talking about people who distinguish themselves and who like to stand out in the crowd. My Dears, first, you must know what you want from your employees, or what you want from a certain person. Don't try to be more eloquent by using the words from the library, no need for that, don't rush things, don't look left-right, just use simple words, a friendly attitude, then clearly and in low tone, distinctly say what you have on your mind. Not everyone is a good speaker, but it doesn't mean that you don't need to work on it as well; everyone knows how to look a person in the eye and send him

a message clearly. Soon enough, you'll see the positive results, and it would be a good base to continue the further improvement in that field.)

BE MAGNIFICENT IN EVERY SENSE.

(Good is not enough, it is actually bad. Pretty good is less bad. Very good is barely passable. Magnificent passes everywhere. It doesn't matter whether it's about your private life or business, do something beyond all the expectations, push every possible boundary, be the one who's setting the standards, have the guts to start up, liberate all the energy, and express your ideas and creativity. No one will complain to that, actually it's something rare; be unique, be one of the rare who accomplish their work magnificently, and then your results will be magnificent as well.)

RECOGNIZE THE LEADERS.

(For a moment, stop admiring yourself and look around you; there are many people like you, and even better than you. How can we recognize the leaders? I'm talking here about all those people who woke up the tiger inside them, and now, they want more, while you and me, we might be too busy to notice it. If you don't recognize them, someone else will and you'll lose a lot. Me, for example, many didn't recognize me, but those who did and who made any kind of cooperation with me, had an interesting and profitable experience, and a good foundation for the future collaboration. I repeat, it doesn't matter on which position in the company that person is working, what is important is *how* he does his job. If you recognize a valuable person, stop that man for a moment, talk to him, advise him which path to take, get close with him, become his mentor if you can, toughen that person, as you'll be tougher too, and if you don't do it, someone else will, and again you'll feel guilty, because you've let go such a person. This already has happened to some people, to me it has, but this is not the reason to let it happen to you too, right?)

CREATE YOUR SUCCESSORS.

(There's no need to be so pretentious and self-confident, all you have to do is to offer a chance and pass the leadership to someone younger and better than you. Naturally, you might not consider him being better than you, but if he's not, then it's your fault, since you hadn't created properly your successor. Creating a successor is a long process, and even when you finally manage to pass the leadership, occasionally it is necessary to check out the things. No one is perfect, you already know that, but it's necessary to aim for perfection. Those who do it, leave magnificent results behind them, one of the impressive ones is the person who resembles you a lot in business, one who does many things the way that you do, one who has even same gestures like yours, only that after all, he's better than you are. Well, my Dears, that magnificent person is your creation, your own product, and this is something that no one can disclaim or deny, not even that man in person; the fact is that everything has started from you, and you will always be there, just in different form—appearance, and everything else will remain the same.

Just to remind you on the advices from this story:

- **LEARN TO LISTEN**

- **LEARN TO MAKE OTHERS LISTEN TO YOU.**

- **BE MAGNIFICENT IN EVERY SENSE.**

- **RECOGNIZE THE LEADERS.**

- **CREATE YOUR SUCCESSORS.**

17

WE ARE ONLY GUESTS
ON THE EARTH

The days and the years are passing much faster than we want them to, and we would do anything to have a chance to occasionally slow, or even stop the time. We think about it when we consider the opportunities we have missed, while those who want more from life think about how they would have more time for completing the legendary goals. Either way, we have only one life and it is necessary to live it the best possible way. What actually is the best possible way? Now, you probably think, "There goes philosophy again". Don't worry, that's not the case. My Dears, it is not enough to apply simply those advices that I gave you to your personal success, it is necessary to share this success. That's right, to share it. You will share it by becoming a useful member of society in every sense. It doesn't matter if it's about your company (then you have even more responsibility) or about an individual, it's very important how you make the relations with people in general, and with the world that you live in.

"We are only guests on the earth", is the sentence pronounced by a simple person, who pronounced it when explaining a certain situation, and who never imagined how this sentence affected me in that moment. When I heard it, it was like the time stopped, everything clicked: the wise

sentence, the occasion, the ambience, the person who pronounced it, why did she pronounced it, and the best of all—I was there to hear it. Some people live tough and cruel lives.

I was visiting an aunt that I hadn't seen in a while. She lives with my uncle in the village, where life is very hard. It is not the kind of village that we see on the movies, that village actually got electricity a couple of years ago, and even today, they don't have bathrooms, and inside the house, they walk on the ground. Many times, she was running away from that house because my uncle was beating her. Naturally, she never spoke about it, but people knew. That was actually considered being a natural behavior, especially if the woman wanted to say something more than YES or NO, then that became a problem. The aunt's health was getting bad, she was suffering from many conditions; when I asked the uncle if he still had problems with the aunt (I translate: if he was still beating her), he said that now she was ill, and that he couldn't beat her since it wasn't alright. You should see the expression on my face when I heard that statement, I looked like Rowan Atkinson (when he makes awkward faces), I was disfigured, but I didn't say a word. My aunt is a simple woman, a housewife, a mother of three, and a very sensible person. In spite of the fact that she didn't even finish the primary school, her every word is well balanced, she speaks without ever raising her voice, and no matter how hard it is for her, she always tries to maintain the happy expression on her face. She was explaining how certain household chore should be done, and how she's attempting to do it properly. Everything she said made a lot of sense, she was constantly repeating how this work has to be done properly, and that all the people involved in that work should be appropriately respected. Afterward, she said that this life is short, and that she's continuously taking care not to offend somebody with her words, because after all, "we are only guests on the earth". I don't remember what she said after that, soon after I stepped out on the fresh mountain air to gather my thoughts.

That woman was, and still is, living in agony, she became ill from a hard work and beatings, yet she always wished to do everything right and not to offend somebody. In addition, she pronounces a sentence with such a deep meaning, a meaning that best describes her fears (to do something bad, or to offend someone), and her hopes, that despite everything, tomorrow will be a better day. Where is the source of her motivation? Where from does she draw that energy? Where is the beauty of her life? Does she know what a normal life is? Does she know in what century she is living? Why hasn't she done some things differently? I know, I know, million questions,

and million weird answers we could get from her, but she gave me all the answers in one sentence, which is probably the source of her motivation. We are only guests on the earth. Would you agree with that?

Can you take any good advices from this story?

I'll try to help you. Here are some advices:

WATCH OUT YOUR WORDS.

(I've already mentioned how necessary it is to maintain the balance in the communication, but here it's about something else. The word is a very powerful weapon. Words start the wars and finish them as well. Words can hurt a lot, both close persons and those that we work with. We all maintain a different image: some are strict, some peculiar and introverted, some are hyperactive, etc; but this is not the reason not to involve the philosophy in your word choice. A nice word opens even an iron door, everybody knows that, but a bad one can close it forever. No need to burn the bridges by saying things you might not even mean. This is very important in business, persons who have good communication skills, as well as those who speak carefully by choosing every word, they are considered being unpredictable. Do you know why? It is because they don't let the tongue run away with their brains. Think about it for a while.)

WATCH OUT YOUR ACTIONS.

(Words and actions are two best friends and two best enemies. How does it work for you? Actions speak a lot (especially in the private life); sometimes they say more than the words do. Them saying more than the words can be efficient and positive, but it can also be a complete disaster. Actions, same as words, have to be restrained and never hasty. I know that sometimes we act impulsively, it is in the human nature, but sometimes we respond with our heart and not with our brain. This type of consequence management can be quite risky in business. Heart in actions replaces the language in words; in business never let your heart speak without a previous consent of the creative side of the brain. It is necessary they cooperate in business, as for your personal life, if you have doubts because of this story, and you don't know whether your should listen to your heart or mind, I cannot

help you with that, I don't wish to give any advices, besides, you must do it alone; as for the business, you've already understood.

PROBLEMS CAN ALWAYS BE BIGGER.

(If you think that you are currently facing the worst possible situation, believe me that you are not; it can always be much worse, because in the times we are living, problems can escalate in even bigger problems, with enormous consequences. What I'm saying now is very important, because small problems, same as the big ones, can paralyze us so much, that we think it's the end of the world. Imagine being beaten several times a week, but every single week, and after a long time, you become ill, and someone then takes pity, and stops beating you since you are ill and he's scared he might beat you to death. It's good when someone decides to stop beating you, but when he decides to continue, and then problems become bigger and much worse. My dear Friends, respect yourself and your parents who took care of you and brought you to this world. No one has the right to destroy your world and to take your life. In business, sometimes we get beaten up, but it is very important not to be beaten twice from the same person. Everybody gets beaten up in business, no matter if badly or not, always someone gets hurt, but if you get punched in the nose twice from the same company, then my Dears, you seem to be the problem, and the big one. Firmly step on the problem, and stop its development, because if you don't, it's simple, in time you will lose everything that you have. The problems can always become bigger, and it's up to you if they actually will.)

LOVE THE LIFE.

(Life is a gift. Life is a magic feeling. Life is an opportunity. Life is a privilege. Life is a most beautiful feeling. Life is one. Life is everything. Is it possible that you don't appreciate all this, and that you are actually doing everything to have a bad life? I don't want to believe it, deep inside everybody appreciates life and its benefits, and all we have to do is wake up and start living. You should be full of life, emit special energy, let know the others that you love living, and that you take life very seriously, because

121

life is one, and you better try to live it in the best possible way. That kind of attitude and behavior will make you become known as person who appreciates life and people, and who sees light even in the great darkness. For a person like this, work represents a challenge and pleasure, and for all the others, this person represents a role model and a prototype of how one should live and treat people. What do you thing, what kind of a role model and prototype is my aunt to her daughters? Do you think that until now, she gave a good example of how life should be lived? How much does she like her life?)

ALWAYS LEAVE GOOD TRACES BEHIND.

(My aunt always left positive impression on me, but that impression was always in the shadow of her decisions and her way of living with my uncle. The fact that she was nice to me once a year, or once in three years, and that she was a good hostess, it doesn't mean that she left good traces behind her. She did, in the way that she paid me respect and served me food, even if they lived in deepest misery, but on the other hand, her way of living and her decisions don't leave good traces behind her. She will always be remembered as a woman who didn't have a strong attitude, who suffered torture, who didn't have the courage to take a new path, and whose decisions affected in major part her children's life as well. If it weren't for that, she would be remembered as a simple and extremely kind person, with true intentions and wishes, always willing to help, and endure all the weight on her back, if needed. Her decisions have put these good qualities in the shadow. My Dears, start thinking of yourself and watch the traces that you leave. What will remain are your children, your company, your name and your surname. Always think about good traces, life will be easier for you, and your successors will have a path with fewer obstacles and difficulties. All the magnificent things are also difficult to achieve, same goes for leaving the good traces, but if you don't aim to that, you will never know how magnificent can be the effects of that practice.

Just to remind you on the advices from this story:

- **WATCH OUT YOUR WORDS.**

- **WATCH OUT YOUR ACTIONS.**

DROP EFFECT

- **PROBLEMS CAN ALWAYS BE BIGGER.**

- **LOVE THE LIFE.**

- **ALWAYS LEAVE GOOD TRACES BEHIND.**

18

I'M BAD AS BEING A SERVANT, IT SUIT ME BETTER TO BE A KING

Everybody gets in awkward situations in life, situations that demand a fast and careful answer that would eventually satisfy both sides and prevent the conflict. We all had conflicts in our lives, some smaller, some bigger, but that is all part of life, and nobody can avoid it. Conflict is a word with a wide meaning, there are many types of conflicts, but here it's about the verbal conflict that could have escalated to a much bigger conflict. I've already mentioned where I work and what is my environment. Times are difficult everywhere, everyone is trying to get his place under the sun in his own way. Sometimes, people don't think, especially those who do illegal business and who use treats and extortions to make profit, and promote themselves as big businesspersons. I always knew what to expect from the criminals, and I was ready for that, but you can never guess what to expect from an ordinary family man. Many criminals don't think this way, but they consider ordinary people as wounded animals, who are easy preys. We all have a survival and defense instinct, some manifest it properly, and others keep it asleep forever. I was hesitating whether I should tell this story

or not, but it represents the best introduction for the advices that will be citing.

I was finishing the diner in my favorite restaurant, at the private table in the bottom of the restaurant, invisible from the main room. I was alone; I didn't want any company, since I was not in a good mood. Many problems and unpredictable situations happened that day, and it disturbed me a lot, but I was trying to stay calm and not to show the tension I was feeling. At the end of the diner, I got a phone call from a pal who said that he needed to see me for five minutes, if possible (it always lasts longer, but never mind). I immediately said that I had a difficult day, and that I was tired, but he insisted. I agreed to see him briefly, and I told him where to come. After the greetings and a ten-minute discussion about irrelevant things, that for some reason is always an introduction for what follows, I told him to cut to the chase and to explain me the reason for his call. He was someone I occasionally see in the center, we chat about irrelevant things and we comment the beautiful girls, and that's it. In the first sentence, he mentioned the person that I don't like to hear about even in a story, and he naively asked me if I had ever heard about him. I told him that I wasn't in the mood for jokes, and that he should cut to the chase.

He said, "Well, my friend, you see that things got a little bit out of control the last months. One close friend of mine heard that this man was asking around about you lately." I asked him, "Why? I didn't know he liked men." He smiled vaguely and continued, "I'm saying all this because I know you, and I wouldn't want that something bad happened to you." I told him to continue. "The story goes like this: you've spread out a lot lately, I know that for you it's not a big of a deal, but certain people see it differently. I'm not talking only about the man that I mentioned, but he's the main character of the story. You've started to attract the attention, you have a driver, bodyguards, and people start to ask what is it about, or should I say, who are you working for? I'm only saying what I heard, I know that you are alone in the business, but that's what people are saying. To make the long story short, since you are tired, the rumor has it, that they already know everything that you do, where you live, where your kids and family spend their time, where you spend most of your time etc. I mean, it's not important, but it shows they know a lot about you. Maybe you should be more careful, and you should reconsider your way of doing business, and

your behavior in general, not to show off that much." I asked him if he has finished, and he confirmed.

"Well, dear friend, I listened to you carefully and I couldn't be more thankful that you are warning me and thinking about me. You don't need to worry, for I would never think that you are involved, or that they are sending you, because you are my friend. That's the first thing. You must understand some things about me, things that you didn't know, and neither did those who are testing me. I could have lost my life already two times, but I'm still here. Every day I wake up and I go to sleep with the worst-case scenario on my mind, so your story didn't surprise me at all. Everything that I've created I can destroy in one day. As for my family, please, seriously no problem, if I only suspected something serious was preparing, they would disappear forever from here; I have thought about it long ago. At the end, it will only be me—an ordinary man who has nothing to lose, a man who has enough money to initiate the same think they initiated, but a man with different way of thinking and different goals. All their intentions will become opportunities for me to send them even a stronger answer. I will simply become their nightmare. Yes, a nightmare, I can say all this to them personally, because I'm not alone, my family is standing behind me, and things will simply be as I told you, and probably even much worse. I know they would like me to be their servant, but I'm a bad servant, I'm a much better king, king of my kingdom, and for other's kingdom I don't care. My friend, it's getting late and it's not the time for heavy words, but we've said them anyway. I know very well, that I'm not a threat to anybody, I didn't deceive anyone, and I didn't do harm to no one. If my presence is bothering someone, he does not need to look when I'm passing. I'm far from being a serious player in business so that I could represent a threat to those people. I'm not saying that I'm irrelevant in business, but all this makes no sense, and I think it's far from being true. Nevertheless, if we suppose that all this is true, then I can say that the damage will be immense on both sides, and that is much more expensive for both of us, and it doesn't serve anyone. I'm not to be tested, but if they wanted to test me with this story, they have my answers, and my past actions say that I'm a man of my word, and that I stand still behind the things that I say and do.

So, was I clear enough?

A bit confused, like he couldn't believe everything he just heard, he said, "Yes, yes, everything is crystal clear." "Very good", I said, "Now you can go and report all this to those that didn't send you, and that you don't have any contact with. Don't even think about denying anything, just go

your way and don't turn around; if I were you, I would do like this, and forget about me and my phone number. The exit is this way, goodbye."

Can you take any good advices from this story?

I'll try to help you. Here are some advices:

ALWAYS CONTROL YOUR EMOTIONS.

(Sometimes, it is very difficult to control the emotions, but this is something you have to deal with. When this conversation happened, I had an especially difficult period in my life, it took place in late hours, which is a big mistake, I didn't control my emotions very well, and I could provoke a real disaster. Usually, when someone mentions your family, you naturally react with your heart, and not with your brain. Slow down, my Dears, slow down, there's always the right place and the right time for everything. That night I made a cardinal mistake, my heart said, probably even, things it didn't mean, (which again is a mistake, you must never do this; always stand behind your words, and never say things that you cannot accomplish). Someone wanted to scare me, and I reacted like a wounded animal, and tried immediately to strike back. That was another mistake. In these kinds of situations, especially when you don't have the complete information, or when you listen to the rumors, you must bite your tongue, sleep on it, and only the next day, when you think it through, you make several options about what you can do. My reaction that night was at least panicky, of course, only the ones who panic and the paranoiacs survive, but in those kinds of situations, they must hold on a bit. These kinds of situations demand, that you concentrate completely on what the other person has to say, and that you try to remember as much as possible from that conversations. Also, remember that those conversations are word plays, and the only important thing is to remember and confirm the very essence of someone's intentions. The details that you hear in-between can help you connect some things, and make you understand better what is going on, the way I understood the intentions of my companion. When you feel most wounded and when you think you will explode, at that moment you should take a deep breath and hold back. If the words in that moment try to come out from your mouth, then you are not controlling your emotions very well, yet if your lips stay calm, and you plan to decide what to say in the morning, then you are in control of your emotions. At the end, it doesn't really matter in which situation you are, controlling your emotions

is a barrier that you simply must have. I have it know, but see what I've been through to start using it.)

NEVER REVEAL YOUR INTENTIONS.

(Another unbelievable mistake, but it occurred in my conversation because I wasn't controlling my emotions. Never, ever reveal your intentions. When you reveal your intentions, the opposite side has a lot of material, and can easily get ready for the attack. In the conversation from the above, there were two sentences pronounced by the other side, which were actually traps for me. A very stupid (that's the right word—stupid) thing for me to do. Not only I swallowed the hook, but also I asked for more. He wanted to test me, to feel and see my fear, and he succeeded at the end. People who react the way I reacted show the fear, regardless what they are saying. Instead, if I've said to him, "Come on, my friend, forget the town gossip, it's not the place nor the time for that, at least you know that I've never hurt anyone, people say many thinks, but who would create problems today when everything can be solved by talking?" If I've acted like that, he would open up more and I would have more information, but instead I told him everything. I explained how I was going to react in that situation, which was a huge mistake, and I made myself even more vulnerable. Keep your plans to yourself, say only enough to bring to an end the awkward situation. My Dears, an hour in the morning is worth two in the evening. We all think differently the day after, but sometimes it can be too late. Be an enigma, be a diplomat, keep the heavy words to yourself, no matter how negative the other person is, try to be even more positive. He will open up and say some unbelievable things.)

ALWAYS THINK ABOUT FIGHTING,
AND NOT ABOUT SURRENDING.

(Don't leave anything to chance, because usually it can cost you a lot. Even if I didn't have the right reaction in this conversation, I took very seriously the words that I've heard, and it was as if they were already knocking on my door. The only advantage in the whole story was that the person I spoke with knew I was a man of my word, that I don't stand the injustice, and that I would never let someone tear me apart without doing something

about it. Naturally, there's always a greater power, and there are always things that I could not deal with, but I would rather burn everything to the ground and start over, just to avoid making even bigger damage for me and for my family. My Dears, we are living in extremely crazy times, where everyone believes they're strong, powerful and that they have full right to what you've been arduously creating. Many think that it's enough to scare you or to blackmail you a bit, and that you will give in. No matter what type of situation this is, no one can take what yours, it's just important to play well the game that is proposed. Do you think it was easy for me to talk like this to this person? Do you think I slept that night? Of course, it was not easy, and of course, I didn't sleep that well. Probably, in your life, you will have a similar situation, a situation where you would be blackmailed in a certain way, or you wouldn't feel secure. I will tell you my opinion: these situations are not about the courage, but about the life philosophy. There are forces we cannot stop, and situations we cannot solve, and we must be ready for this. If you are willing to succumb under pressure, then you better immediately find a local criminal and offer him everything you own, so you won't be having any trouble in the future. If you are willing to respect yourself, your work, your life, and your family, then every power, no matter how big, will have trouble to take what you've built. Even if it does take it, you won't be surrendering without a fight, and it says a lot about you, and your life philosophy. You cannot know where the danger will come from, but you can know that you won't surrender without a fight, and that's more than enough for the start.)

EXCHANGE THE ROLES; YOU WILL LEARN MORE.

(We all communicate differently, and it's only a question of how ready we are in certain situations, to adapt ourselves to someone's way of communicating. Investors have their language, lawyers have a different one, government clerks speak in their own, and the criminals speak in a different one. Can you adapt yourself to their way of communicating, and keep the balance in the communication? It is very important that you are familiar with different ways of communication. You have your way of negotiating, but sometimes you need to adapt yourself and to understand their way of thinking. I had a chance to have conversations with different people, and I took many advices. In the above-mentioned conversation, I've made a mistake because I've started to speak like "my friend" or should I say, like

people who had sent him, and there was no need for that. You need to understand what is crucial in the conversation, and to recognize the critical moments in negotiations, because if you make a mistake, those could escalate into a big problem. When you find yourself facing the problem, choose your terms carefully, and don't try to understand other people's words in your own way, but in the way of the person who had pronounced them. It is necessary to put yourself in the other person's position, and things will appear much more understandable. It doesn't matter what kind of situation it is about, if you get confused, just put yourself in the other person's shoes, and ask yourself what would be the best way to take what I want from this man? In the unpleasant conversation that I had, I revealed too much information, and it's my fault that I didn't exchange the roles for a moment, and asked myself certain questions. It always helps me to put myself in other person's shoes, because in that way, I have myself in front of me, and I try to make million tricky questions so I can understand, and get what I want. Whenever I exchange the roles, first I always ask myself what is the main reason, why did he choose me, and not someone else. Start with that, you will get magnificent results.)

BE READY TO BURN EVERYTHING DOWN

(I don't want to connect this to my story, but just tell me, how often you think about the possibility to remain without anything, and to burn everything down. It is very hard to renounce to everything that you have been creating for years and decades, I know this very well, but would you give it to someone without a fight, or you rather burn everything to the ground, so that he wouldn't have a reason to spend time on you. My Dears, don't get me wrong, I'm not referring to everything that you've created, sometimes it's only about an individual project or something personal; the question is how much strength you have to burn down everything, and start from the scratch. Only the thought of it is terrifying enough, but believe it or not, this is one of the best ways of doing business. Always have a backup plan when you run your business (remember the advice on good husbandry), so if someone puts pressure on you, or if the global financial crisis happens, be ready to burn everything to the ground, and to have the strength to go on. Man is stronger than the rock, he can endure and carry on a great deal, but it is very important to be persistent in your intentions, and to organize your business that way. I compliment the fact that you want to

build your company, that you value the tradition and blah, blah, blah . . . However, what will happen if you lose your compass, and by trying to save your company, you actually put your family in jeopardy? Why does your family have to pay for you being in the wrong bus, and not controlling well your emotions? That's why it is essential to think about this as well; we are only humans made of flesh and blood, and we'll make mistakes as long as we live. So, if you make a mistake, put a gentle/wise smile on your face and say, "I wasn't lucky this time, let's move on." Every time you burn something down, everything that follows will be much better and much more efficient, you'll be richer in experience; I'm saying all this, I repeat, from my personal experience. Do not get married with your company (it's enough that you've got married with your wife); the company is here today and gone tomorrow, the family is always here and it has to remain this way. Make a choice.)

Just to remind you on the advices from this story:

- **ALWAYS CONTROL YOUR EMOTIONS.**

- **NEVER REVEAL YOUR INTENTIONS.**

- **ALWAYS THINK ABOUT FIGHTING, AND NOT ABOUT SURRENDING.**

- **EXCHANGE THE ROLES; YOU WILL LEARN MORE.**

- **BE READY TO BURN EVERYTHING DOWN**

19

HOT & COLD, FIRE & WATER, BLACK & WHITE

Does it ever seem to you that all the knowledge and experience that you have, are not even close to be enough in certain situations? Is there any strategy in communicating that could buy you time during the negotiations, so you could find the real strategy and close the deal to your advantage? Many times, during the negotiations, both sides look at each other a little bit confused, and you don't know which way the negotiation is going. Every client is a different story, but sometimes we run up into a real enigma of a client, where it really takes a miracle to wake him and make him say one word. There are times, when it's not a wise silence from his side, but a complete absence, or apathy, or something else. No matter how experienced we are in business, we can see things about the client, but we are far from being psychic to know everything about him, or what is it that he wants. Many people give advices on how to persuade the client that your product is the right one, that you product is essential, that it is exactly what your client actually needs, that you are a highly regarded company, and blah, blah, blah, blah. I had many difficult negotiations until now, yet the most difficult ones where in time when I needed money emergently. It is very important how you react in those situations, whether you are cold

when it's very hot, and if you are black when everything is white (and the other way around), in other words, how well you balance other people's feelings, and how well do you hide having problems that had to be solved "yesterday".

A couple of months have passed, my company was deep in debts, and we couldn't manage to sell even one apartment. At the beginning, we were refusing every offer we had, for they all seemed unreal and unacceptable at that time. When the situation became alarming, and when the expenses started to grow, while the income failed to follow, I realized that I should have considered more the offers I had been given, but there was no way back. I was looking at the financial reports in my office and I truly didn't know which way to turn. It seemed to me I was sinking, and that there was no way out this time. I was not panicking, but I had a difficult time; after all, I had over 70 employees at that time, as well as two projects halfway to completion. While I was considering the options in my office, I got a phone call from one of my workers who said we had some buyers for an apartment, and he asked if I was free to see them, since they explicitly wanted to speak with me. At that moment the situation was so difficult that I would have gone to them, but naturally, I said that I needed to check my schedule, and that my secretary will call back. After 15 minutes, the secretary informed them that I was only available tomorrow at 12 o'clock; she asked them to be on time, since it was not common for the General Manager of the company to meet the clients, but I made an exception as they insisted. I prolonged my agony for another day, even if I could see them in that very moment. The next morning, the financial situation in my company got even worse, I had two unplanned meetings, and that entire crowd almost made me forget about the meeting that could save me in the last moment. The buyers were on time, I received them in the congress room. They were four, and immediately I presumed that one of them was an attorney and the other a real estate agent. The attorney, like every attorney—very full of himself, was judging the premises with pretentious looks, while the buyers were patiently waiting for the meeting to start. I welcomed them, and after the refreshments were served, I asked them naively the reason for their coming, moreover, which apartment was it about. Naturally, I had the complete information from the field; however, I had to respect my order of negotiating. The real estate agent explained everything well, the buyers didn't say a word, while the attorney was waiting for his turn to state his real opinion. After their speeches, which are less relevant in this moment, it was the buyers' turn to speak. Mr. Client said that they liked the apartment,

but they didn't have enough money. They've sold a house, and now they have to buy two apartments. The apartment was gorgeous, but they were short of a certain amount of money. Then, they waited for my reaction, which was something like, "Go on, I'm listening carefully". "Times are difficult, our country is facing crisis, we're talking about big amount of money, we've seen many apartments, we have another two offers, but we came here to see what your company can offer." I must admit, my Dears, that I heard million similar stories, but the gentleman that spoke to me was a real enigma, he never mentioned the key words that would give me more security and hope that we're about to close the deal. My turn came to speak. Long time ago, my Dears, I learned the game hot-cold, you've all heard of it, but this one regards the negotiations. Even today, I'm improving myself in that game, and I probably will as long as I live, but I started to make good use of it. The strategy, that I call game, is very dangerous and when you use it, you are actually walking on the edge, because you are directly caressing and hitting the client's ego, and in this case, the attorney and the agent were present as well. I'm not producing insulin or any kind of fuel to be indispensible, and for buyers not to have another option, I'm building apartments, and there are hundreds everywhere, so buyers can avoid me whenever they want, which doesn't put me in such a great position. I have to be much more careful, since I have a tough competition, and there's not much space for pretentiousness and arrogance. Since I'm always aware of it, I do the negotiations on the edge, yet with full respect of the client, and his complete entourage in this case.

"Dear Gentlemen, I listened carefully to what each of you had to say, so I will answer you in the same order. Mr. Agent, I've heard about your agency, you are on the market for a long time, and you are well known (hot), but what you are selling, I'm making (cold), so that makes me present from the birth of the product, and maybe, just maybe, I'm familiar with the subject matter a little bit better than you are (cold). I agree with you on many things, I see you know very well the circumstances and the competition (hot), but each company is different, and it's also the case with this one (cold). As I have the opportunity to follow the world trends, both in services and production, I can say that our product is highly rated on the market (cold), but you've already mentioned that you had heard about us, and that you are familiar with our work methods (cold). For the above-mentioned reasons, there's no need to use different techniques for discovering the inexistent flaws. Mr. Attorney, I heard about your firm, you represented a friend of mine (a big plastic production factory)

who was very satisfied with your services (hot). You declared that papers were "mostly fine" and that you "don't have many remarks". You have to know, that people who are present here are using their last money to buy an apartment, and that is practically all they have (I was making a "hot" introduction for the buyers), and the least they like to hear is something is "mostly fine" or "don't have many remarks". Mister, you know that a girl cannot be a little pregnant, she's pregnant or she's not, there's not midpoint (laughter in the conference room), however (cold) same goes here, papers are either fine or they're not." He was just about to interrupt me, like every attorney does, but I stopped him. "Let me continue, I would never do this job if I hadn't previously consulted the law. The truth is our law has many ambiguities, imprecision and holes, which you explained pretty well, since it is very important in our business (hot), and particularly in yours, but if you look a little bit better, you will see that our papers are made under the law, and that you have probably used the wrong expression (cold). You've already said that well composed papers, like these, were rarity in our country (hot), so then, it means, not probably, but certainly that everything is all right, do you agree with me?" "Well ok, you're right, everyone interprets the law in a different way, I had to bring all the details to my clients' intention, but all right, we can continue," declared the attorney a bit angrily. I thanked him. "Dear Gentlemen (the buyers), I can see that you are thorough and cautious in business, which I approve a lot (hot), because when you appear like this with an attorney and an agent, you spread panic in some companies, but here it's not the case, as you can see (cold). I understand your situation and I listened very carefully to what you had to say. You heard from the agent and the attorney that everything is under the law, from their side, and they don't have any objections that you become my buyer. I must tell you that the apartment that you chose is remarkable, it shows that you know what you want (hot), but also it shows that you are unreasonable when it comes to reducing the price (cold). That is quite natural, you came on openly to me, and you presented everything that you have, that is fair from you (hot), but I think that we bumped into insurmountable obstacle, because I'm not at all ready to negotiate the price, especially since it's already on a discount. I'm begging you to slow down for a moment, and to think through all the facts that you heard today, and only then make the decision. You don't buy an apartment every day, it's a big decision and you must not hurry (while I'm in such a hurry that I'm about to explode). I repeat the apartment is exceptional indeed, especially the view on the city, the silence, the park behind it, simply it's

that good that there is nothing more to add, but I'm so sorry that you cannot afford it, since I can see that you really like it a lot. I suggest the best thing to do is to wait for couple of days, and we can speak again, and see your decision then. "This is the best thing to do", said the agent, "but until then you could sell it to someone else." "That's true, it had happen to me several times, but that's business, isn't it?" "That's all very nice, but how can we spend so much money when we hadn't planned to", said the buyer's wife. "Dear Gentlemen, this meeting is getting too long, I'll give you my last price (and previously I didn't want to discuss the price), and if you accept it, you must know that you made a great deal." When I pronounced the final price, which was fair enough, the buyers looked at each other and became even more indecisive. What a nightmare, and I was starting to feel dizzy. Then the husband said that he would accept, but only if I accepted to pay the court fees and taxes, as well as the attorney's fees (which was actually an insignificant amount comparing to the price of the apartment). "I'm sorry Gentlemen, I cannot accept that, and this is not my habit (cold), but (a dramatic pause, like I'm thinking of something, while I already decided what to offer if actually came to that), hum . . . maybe I could offer you something else. Excuse me, but the court fees are not worth mentioning, and it is more than enough that I have to overpay my own attorney, I really couldn't start paying yours as well (a small relaxation like introduction to the final offer). Since you know that one department of my company does the interior renovation, I could arrange for you to choose different colors for your walls, and my painters will paint your apartment. That is something we hardly ever do, but this service will be involved in the arranged price like a form of value added to your purchase. This means that, not only you get an apartment, but also something more. What do you say, do we have a deal?" The smile said everything, and after that, we all felt very hot, the coldness disappeared.

Can you take any good advices from this story?

I'll try to help you. Here are some advices:

LEARN YOUR JOB WELL.

(It doesn't matter if you are owner of the company, or just an employee, it is crucial that you know your job to the details, as well as the company work. Those who know a lot about the company, about its way of doing business and about people who lead it, they tend to stand out in the crowd.

When, in time, you become good in what you do, your skills upgrade to the next level, while some surprise situations become actually your everyday routine. Yes, it's like that, but it happens only for those who make an effort to develop their working skills, and make better business results with it. My job is to know everyone's job in my company, which I hope won't prevent me from staying more or less sane, at least in the close future. Employees who see your company with your eyes are very rare, and it always represents a problem. I don't know if it's your case too, but I had to pass through all the levels in my company. I had long meetings with accountants, lawyers, engineers, government clerks, etc; I saw there were many things regarding my business that I didn't know, and I was trying to learn the most important. In time, I became so good, that I managed to maintain a dialogue with the previously mentioned people, and to communicate on a higher level with them. Don't let yourself be unprepared, and don't permit not knowing all the details about your business. Master the subject matter, and upgrade yourself continuously in your business field. You already know all the things that I wrote in this advice, but some of you tend to forget, to fall asleep, and some let the time pass them by. That's why there are people who do their job well (which is confirmed by their results), and those who just do their job (who work for completing other people's results). For the start, it's enough to learn your job, and to always know what you are talking about (even there, many get lost); this is one of the tools for the accomplishment of the top results. Those who do their job well know what I'm talking about, and those who just do their job, know it even better.)

EVERY SURPRISE DEMANDS SPECIAL ATTENTION.

(No matter how big problem this might cause you, you need to react with special attention on every surprise. No matter who is coming to the business meeting, or how many persons came unexpectedly, you must always act as it is not a problem for you, as if it's just a daily routine; but on the other hand, you need to be concentrating yourself completely on a possibility of the drop effect. Many of you would say, "I don't care how many persons come to a meeting; for me, that's not a problem." I know, my Dears, that is not a problem for you, this is why this book is entitled *Drop Effect*, so you can understand this meeting could be a problem for you, and that it could take more of your time than expected, because more people came,

and you didn't plan it. Besides, because of that, you will be forced to move other meetings, and you don't know the kind of reactions this will produce; this is the drop effect in action. If you take the surprise too lightly, there's a big possibility of widening the unplanned things, and drowning in the drops. Every surprise requires a special approach and attention, a full concentration and to look as if you were not surprised. I believe that the attorney and the real estate agent from my story thought, considering my reaction, that I didn't notice them so well, and that I did not care they came. That thinking gave them the strength to attack. I noticed very well all the persons who came, and I recognized the attorney and the agent even before their introduction. The truth is that they really attacked me, but they didn't expect such an efficient counterattack, and this only for one reason, they took me for an ordinary thing, and not as a surprise that demands a special approach and attention. Dear Friends, be careful of these things, everyone is a surprise, everyone needs a special approach, and the one who doesn't think this way, simply gets surprised and defeated.)

THE COMMUNICATION IS CRUCIAL WHEN NEGOTIATING.

(In my case, it definitely is, and this applies for many companies that are not monopolistic or indispensable. We live in crazy times, having so many options, we tend to get indecisive sometimes. In our era people have everything; the product quality is almost equalized, as well as the technology and the design. How can we choose when everything seems so attractive and top-rate? What is the thing that would eventually outweigh in your decision to buy an apartment from me or from my opponent, if the buildings were identical? First, the way that we would approach you, in other words, the communication that has the major role in the negotiations, plus the value added to the purchased product. Adding value to a product or a service helps finalizing the negotiation. You should keep it as backup, in case the buyer's eye starts focusing the door and not you. The key is the communication, my Dears. However, are we all able to be great communicators? What is the thing that outweighed in the negotiation with my buyers? It's my attitude, my way of treating them, primary as my guests, and then as buyers as well; what outweighed was my knowledge, my way of listening, and my communication. For the start, it's enough to talk to the buyers and clients the way that you would want someone to talk to you.

When you realize you are on the right path, then switch to the game hot & gold, which is described in the next two advices.)

WARM UP THE OTHER PERSON'S EGO.

(Always start the game hot & cold with worm words, specifically with words that are caressing the other person's ego. No one likes the sharpness, the speed, the bad words, and similar, on the other hand, no matter the outcome of the meeting, everyone appreciates when being respected, and when you act fairly in negotiation and business. Everybody likes to be complimented within moderation for they work and their achievements (don't overdo it, they will notice), this always has to be your first step when starting the negotiation. You can see from my story, that I was attempting to reach the other persons with mild compliments, I tried to let them know that I was familiar with their work or their profession, that I respect what they do, and that I estimate their presence. Pretentiousness and arrogance always have a counter effect in these situations, and no one benefits from them. So, my dear Friends, first you have to warm the ego of the other person, and just when he starts feeling your mild submission, then it is the time to cool him down a bit, just to create balance; and this is the next advice.)

COOL DOWN THE OTHER PERSON'S EGO.

(All the nice things have an end, so does the warming of someone's ego. People tend to overestimate themselves, tend to think what they did no one ever did before or will ever do. They usually show it with an overconfident attitude, and arrogant way of communicating in the negotiations. A nice word opens even an iron door, it is essential to improve atmosphere by warming up the other person's ego, however immediately in the next sentence, with the same tone of voice, but with a different sigh, cool down his ego, so that you can take off his face the smile he is not showing. You can see from my story that each cooling of the ego was equally strong as the warming. You must avoid sharp words and bragging. Stick to the subject matter, and try to create balance, but I recommend it to be a positive balance. Cooling down helps putting the other person in his place, making him understand who's in front of him, who is the person he's dealing with, but

nothing more than that. Cooling down is not a tool in negotiations meant for rubbing someone's nose or making fun of somebody, it's just meant to help you turn the situation in your advantage, and nothing else. Play the game until you disarm the other person, but always finish with a mild warming of the ego, because everyone gathered there to finish something positive, and this is what should outweigh in the end, the positivity.)

ALWAYS, BE THE ONE TO START, AND THE ONE TO FINISH.

(The introduction and the closing speeches mean very much, lawyers know it the best. The introduction speech is an introduction in the problem situation; it's like an entrance ticket to a safari, but the closing speech is like an oasis, an oasis that you have to discover, an oasis where you'll let everyone drink the water. Your closing speech has to be exactly like this. Everybody is thirsty and hungry of something, like in my story, the ordinary people just wanted to make a good deal and solve their life problem. My oasis seemed nice to them, even if there were many oases in the area, they stopped by in this one, and here is where they finally quenched their thirst. The closing speech can say much more than all the other words said at the meeting, and it can be the key for closing the deal. Always be the one to finish the meeting, show your respect for the last time to all the present people, regardless the outcome of the meeting. Even if you didn't succeed to come to an agreement, your behavior and your way of communicating will leave the impression of you being a professional and fair person (which you are), who didn't have a possibility to be flexible enough to make a deal to both sides satisfaction. Nevertheless, those persons will leave your premises with positive impressions, and this is the only feeling they could have about you and your company.)

Just to remind you on the advices from this story:

- **LEARN YOUR JOB WELL.**

- **EVERY SURPRISE DEMANDS SPECIAL ATTENTION.**

- **THE COMMUNICATION IS CRUCIAL WHEN NEGOTIATING.**

- **WARM UP THE OTHER PERSON'S EGO.**

- **COOL DOWN THE OTHER PERSON'S EGO.**

- **ALWAYS, BE THE ONE TO START, AND THE ONE TO FINISH.**

20

WISDOM IS THE CRADLE OF PAIN

Dear Gentlemen, many of the stories have been told in this book and many have not. This chapter does not contain a life story or any advices. This chapter's title is heavy enough, and I don't know if all my life stories would be enough to explain and describe myself. I wanted to put all my thoughts on a paper, and to share them with the rest of the world, which I did. I tried to summarize all the stories efficiently enough to give you the advices that could help you in your further personal and professional improvement. The writing conditions were not the best, but when I made the decision, there was no turning back. From day to day, the subtitles were following one another, and all I had to do, is spare enough time to put on the paper all my thoughts.

At the moment, I'm doing more than a few things, I'm starting on a couple of new projects, I'm attempting to spend enough time with my family, and the rest of the time, I spend on writing this book. While writing I try to concentrate completely, but sometimes my thoughts wonder off. However, even if I wonder off a million times, this won't erase the history and the magnificent mistakes that I had made. Life stories can be different, but each of us takes out a different message from his personal life story, or should I say, from his personal mistakes. Now that I'm writing the last story,

I'm deeply convinced that I'm doing the right thing, because every story, every advice is written honestly and from the heart, and I hope that after reading this book, you will feel it as well. I was hesitating whether I should write a book like this, after all I was speaking openly about my life and my experiences, but while I'm writing this last story, I have this incredible feeling of happiness, because I know I didn't make a mistake. Some of us will continue the same way, while others, like me, will stop, open their eyes and think thoroughly where to go from here. Do you really think that I know with certainty where to go from here? Of course I don't, but I have the path composed of my mistakes—life lessons that largely illuminate the road that I'm about to pass. Does it mean that I won't be making any more mistakes, at least not the same ones? Naturally, it doesn't; I will make many more mistakes, but I'm not the same person anymore, now things will be different when I face the challenges. The point is to take a lesson from the mistakes that you've made; it would largely help you accomplish both your personal and professional goals.

I like to say that it's a mistake only when you repeat the same wrong thing; but when you see what kind of consequences came from the certain situations, and then you realize that even the first one was—a mistake. There are stories I didn't tell, but I discussed many advices that could prepare you for the stories unmentioned in this book. You're probably wondering now, how come you are so good that you have universal advices? Of course, I don't, but many advices will help avoid certain situations that could make permanent consequences. Some situations actually create scars on our lives, and often we fall asleep, and wake up, thinking of them. That's why it's essential to measure twice and to make wise decisions. Many will ask, what is actually the wisdom? How can we define it? I would also like to ask many similar questions.

Dear Friends, I was always saying that it takes years to acquire the wisdom, and it's a path filled with obstacles; almost everybody is on that path, it's just that some are faster, and others slower, some never reach the end, and others never even find themselves on that path. Wisdom is a heavy word and must not be used casually. It could be considered as a phenomenon holding the answers to all the life secrets. It's up to us to overmaster this phenomenon, but even if we had three lives, again we would fail the simplest exam. A set of different consequences makes an ordinary man get off the right path and doesn't let him discover so fast all the life secrets. If we eventually manage to get back on the right path, it means that we'll have one more experience that is valuable; however, there would be a

thousand more temptations on which we'll have to pass the test. Naturally, dear Friends, I don't want to offend those who consider themselves being wise people, it's a privilege, it's a gift; all I do is try to share my thoughts, and give directions for all those who still haven't entered that society. We spend our whole life upgrading the knowledge and the experience, and with years, we truly become wiser than we were in the beginning, but sometimes, even at the end, we make mistakes that not even a five year old would make. Why is it so? We think we are these perfect beings, unique in a magnificent way. Certain individuals open their eyes from time to time and realize where they are, and then, they take a deep breath and enter bravely the battle, but what about the others? Well, nothing, they just follow the mentioned individuals. Those individuals decided to make big sacrifices and to endure a lot of pain to be able to do things the way it's good for them, and for those around them. Those individuals travel on an unfamiliar path, they won't be wounded again in the same places, but they don't fear further fighting and new wounds, because they know it's the only way to discover something new, which will make this world a better place. I recommend you do the same: keep on lasting, on existing, on making the world a better place, on living, because you have only one opportunity for life, it's an incredible privilege and gift, while there are a thousand opportunities for the job, it's not a privilege or a gift, it's something that gives meaning to life. That's why it is not enough that you've decided to live, the decision has to have a meaning, and that meaning is to be found in continuous work and improvement. There is a lot of truth in everything that you read, however one truth is certain: the path of discovering the secrets of wisdom is the cradle of pain.

In the end, I have to ask you to be careful about the drops. They seem so small and meaningless, yet the "drop effect" can be so big and meaningful, but you already know it well after reading this book. I wish you all the best.

ABOUT THE AUTHOR

Now in his early thirties Milan Dimitrijevic is founder and the owner of private consulting company engaged in several lines of business, its primary activities include project management, construction investment , projects of mergers and acquisitions, international investment and relations, change management consulting , for legal entities, private investors and celebrities. He obtained his master's and PHD degree in Strategic Management from Alfa University in Belgrade. He is a Professor at the Faculty for Management in Novi Sad, Serbia (www.famns.edu.rs) in the Department of Management.

He is the author of the books: *Introduction to Strategic Management, Introduction to Public Relations and Public Relations for management engineers.* He is the organizer, the main lecturer of the seminars entitled Change Management, and Communication Ability held for medium and top management in big companies and corporations.

Dimitrijevic is a member and fellow worker of the prestigious CIPR Institute for public relations from London (www.cipr.co.uk) as well as the Strategic Management Society from Chicago (www.strategimanagement. net). He is a Member of Honor and fellow worker of the Engineering Management Society of Serbia (www.dims.rs).

Milan Dimitrijevic is also a dedicated philanthropist and President of the Board of the Dimitrijevic Foundation (www.fondacijadimitrijevic. com), whose primary goals are directed in providing aid to sick children, children without parents, as well as to most endangered families in Serbia.

For more information visit:
www.milandimitrijevic.com

www.ingramcontent.com/pod-product-compliance
Lightning Source LLC
Chambersburg PA
CBHW020238290526
45784CB00003B/1021